MENTORING EACH OTHER

Teachers listening, learning, and sharing to create more successful classrooms

Lana Parker | Diane Vetter

Pembroke Publishers Limited

538 Hood Road
Markham, Ontario, Canada L3R 3K9
www.pembrokepublishers.com

Library and Archives Canada Cataloguing in Publication

Title: Mentoring each other : teachers listening, learning, and sharing to create more successful classrooms / Lana Parker, Diane Vetter.

Names: Parker, Lana, author. | Vetter, Diane, author.

Identifiers: Canadiana (print) 20200194658 | Canadiana (ebook) 20200194739 | ISBN 9781551383460 (softcover) | ISBN 9781551389455 (PDF)

Subjects: LCSH: Mentoring in education.

Classification: LCC LB1731.4 .P37 2020 | DDC 371.102dc23

Editor: Kat Mototsune
Cover Design: John Zehethofer
Typesetting: Jay Tee Graphics Ltd.

Printed and bound in Canada
9 8 7 6 5 4 3 2 1

Contents

Introduction

As teachers who have worked with students in K–12 schools and adult education, teacher candidates in preservice education, and new teachers entering the profession, we came to realize that formal preparation for the role of mentor is often not readily available. For teachers who are leading professional practice in their schools by working with preservice or novice teachers, we recognize that the role of mentor may not be clearly defined. Teachers with a few years of experience and a willingness to open their classroom doors may be taking on the role of host, associate, or collaborating teacher with only a school board or faculty of education handbook to guide their way. Many of the teachers we met while we researched mentoring indicated that, in taking on the role of supporting a new colleague or preservice teacher, they did not actually think of themselves as mentors.

Mentoring is a complex process and each mentor/mentee relationship is unique. These relationships function within an education environment that meets the specific requirements of the district and reflects the diversity of school communities. The process of mentoring generally happens within the confines of a busy school day. That means that time is a precious commodity and that making good use of that time is key to a successful mentoring experience for both mentor and mentee.

Mentoring Each Other: Teachers Listening, Learning, and Sharing to Create More Successful Classrooms is written to support the dedicated teaching professionals who are continually seeking to improve their practice, for both the children in their classrooms and the teachers of tomorrow they mentor. It provides accessible and practical strategies that can be easily implemented to support and enhance the mentoring and learning process.

Our work and research in education has led us to the understanding that becoming and being a teacher and mentor is multifaceted and dynamic. It involves relationship-building, knowledge and skills development, reciprocal learning, leadership, and community. Our research in the area of mentoring advances the concept of mentoring as a shared process that considers a reciprocal dynamic, teacher leadership, and collaborative learning within community. We offer the reader a new perspective on mentoring and the role of the mentor, along with tools to support mentoring as an inquiry-based, shared endeavor that values equity, telling our stories, and relationship-building.

We believe that mentoring capacity and teacher growth are linked by several common elements:

- Honest self-reflection
- Openness to listening and sharing
- Willingness to make professional practices and vulnerabilities public
- Recognition of the value of reciprocal and active learning
- Collaboration within professional communities that adapt and change as learning evolves

This book addresses the questions, opportunities, and challenges that teachers face in their mentoring relationships and classroom practice. Embedded in its chapters are relevant and purposeful Mentoring Moves, very specific tools and strategies that can be used to support mentoring and to develop reflective practice. They were developed as a targeted response to teachers' comments and questions that appeared in our research. Mentoring Moves are practical and easily implemented in daily practice. Some of these Mentoring Moves are known education strategies that we have adapted to mentoring contexts; others are original ideas we have implemented in our research and used successfully in our work with mentors and mentees over the past few years.

The chapters in this book can be read sequentially or accessed according to the area of need that emerges within the professional context. This overview will give you an idea of where to seek out the information you need.

In Chapter 1 we consider relationship-building as foundational to The Mentoring Partnership, specifically addressing the following questions:

- What does it mean to be a mentor? (See page 9.)
- What does the process of mentoring look like? (See page 12.)
- How does mentoring differ from modelling? (See page 16.)
- What attributes best support the role of mentor? (See page 19.)
- How might we build trust in a mentoring relationship? (See page 23.)
- What do mentees expect of their mentors? (See page 25.)

In Chapter 2 we take a close look at Knowledge and Skills Development as a process of shared learning, and consider the following questions:

- How might I articulate my philosophies of education and my practice as a teacher? (See page 36.)
- How might I share what I know? (See page 39.)
- How might I make visible to a mentee the thinking and rationale that underpin my teaching? (See page 42.)
- How might I communicate effective feedback on classroom practices and processes? (See page 45.)
- How might I support mentees in self-assessing skills development? (See page 48.)
- How might I help mentees identify their specific needs? (See page 52.)

In Chapter 3 we reflect on new ways of thinking about mentoring as an experience of Reciprocal Learning, to discuss the following questions:

- How and why might we transition from the traditional expert/novice roles to partners in learning? (See page 62.)
- How might the mentoring partnership respond to the unique needs and qualities of the mentor and mentee? (See page 64.)

- How might we make the mentoring experience mutually rewarding and beneficial? (See page 66.)
- How might mentoring support productive risk-taking to facilitate growth? (See page 69.)
- How might we negotiate difference? (See page 71.)
- How might action research and inquiry facilitate mentor and mentee professional learning? (See page 75.)

In Chapter 4 we look at Mentoring as Leadership, raising the following questions:

- How might opening my classroom door demonstrate leadership? (See page 86.)
- How might I cultivate a space for open minds? (See page 89.)
- How might we navigate challenging conversations? (See page 91.)
- How might documentation for professional growth and development support leadership? (See page 94.)
- How might I lead learning? (See page 96.)
- How might mentoring serve as a catalyst for additional leadership roles in education? (See page 99.)

Finally, in Chapter 5 we discuss Creating a Mentoring Community, bringing the action of mentoring beyond the classroom, with a focus on the following questions:

- Why should we endeavor to form mentoring communities? (See page 109.)
- How might we begin to build a mentoring community? (See page 112.)
- How might storytelling contribute to mentoring communities? (See page 114.)
- How might witnessing strengthen partnerships? (See page 117.)
- How might mentoring communities enable progress toward school and system goals? (See page 119.)
- How might the strategies I use with my mentoring community be implemented with the students in my classroom? (See page 122.)

We trust that that our Mentoring Moves and the stories we share will be valuable to teachers as they continue on their journey to teaching excellence and as they mentor those teachers whose journey is just beginning.

1

The Mentoring Partnership

Mentoring can be challenging. In our experience, all mentees are sincere in their desire to achieve the objectives set out for them. In order to do so, they need a mentor who will commit to the task of mentoring, even when times get tough. This takes patience and compassion on the part of a mentor who must maintain their objectivity and communicate with the mentee in an honest and forthright manner. They must also communicate with enough empathy and sensitivity to avoid demoralizing the mentee, who may already be overwhelmed or fearful when things are not going smoothly.

Mentors may also be called upon to act as counsellors who raise a mentee's morale or remind them to inventory their strengths and abilities when they feel challenged by the demands of the profession. In all cases, it is not the task of the mentor to be the answer to a mentee's problem or to be the lifeline that saves the mentee from a difficult situation. Rather, the mentor needs to support the mentee in unleashing their own power to make the necessary changes to move from struggle to success.

Relationship-building is a complex process. All relationships function on both a conscious and a subconscious level. Within the mentoring process, this means that there will be elements of the relationship that mentor and mentee actively understand and control; other elements that affect the relationship might lie below their conscious understanding. For example, the mentor and mentee may share common interests or personal backgrounds that lead to a natural affinity whose roots can be identified. On the other hand, subconscious elements, perhaps resulting from experiences or relationships no longer part of your conscious memory—such as a past relationship with a great teacher…or a not so great teacher—can also have an impact on the mentoring relationship.

To support mentors and mentees in navigating this complex relationship process, we have identified a series of relational aspects to facilitate success. We begin by visualizing a **mentoring disposition** that is central to the role of mentoring. We look at the relationship as being underpinned by a **mentoring process** that sets parameters within which the relationship unfolds. To support relationship-building within the partnership, we make explicit the difference between **modelling and mentoring**. We examine the **attributes** that might cultivate a positive mentoring experience. Then we explore the element of **trust** that grows between collaborators. Finally, we acknowledge that within this relationship, there will always be **expectations** to be recognized and clarified.

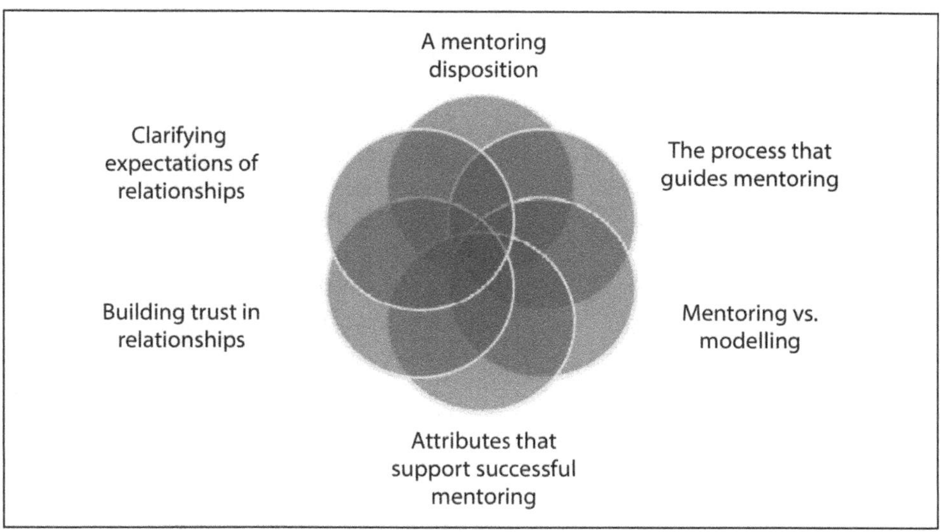

To address these mentoring relationship topics we consider these key questions:

- What does it mean to be a mentor? (See page 9.)
- What does the process of mentoring look like? (See page 12.)
- How does mentoring differ from modelling? (See page 16.)
- What attributes best support the role of mentor? (See page 19.)
- How might we build trust in a mentoring relationship? (See page 23.)
- What do mentees expect of their mentors? (See page 25.)

What does it mean to be a mentor?

A Mentoring Disposition

The Oxford Reference dictionary explains the origin of the word *mentor*:

> In Greek mythology and Homer's Odyssey, Mentor was the guide and counsellor for Odysseus's son Telemachus. Educators and others have adopted the word to describe a formal or informal attachment between a teacher and a student or small group of students that goes beyond mere teaching or tutoring to include advice and guidance about many other issues and problems encountered by students.

We love that this definition identifies the importance of attachment (what we refer to as *relationship*) in mentoring, along with the understanding that mentoring extends beyond "mere teaching or tutoring." While a mentor may share knowledge and demonstrate skills, a true mentoring disposition moves the mentor to support mentees in broader ways.

Stories from the Field: Seeing Ourselves as Mentors (Lana and Diane)

When we began working with mentors, we were surprised to hear that most of the teachers we spoke to did not think of their role as mentoring. Many saw themselves as giving back to the profession or paying forward an experience from their own days as preservice teachers. A few indicated they felt compelled by an administrator. Many teachers who had taken on the teaching-and-tutoring role saw themselves as experienced teachers with something to share with the teachers of tomorrow, but they did not consider themselves to be mentors.

Working with preservice or new colleagues, most experienced teachers felt they had few resources to rely on. To undertake their roles, they generally reflected on what had helped them when they were joining the profession, what host teachers in their past experience had or had not done to support the experience, and what just seemed right. Most often, those mentoring a colleague simply thought of themselves as teachers supporting other teachers, without naming their valuable role as mentoring.

We believe that all teachers supporting preservice, novice, or experienced teachers are mentors. Our research demonstrates that the mentors we encountered wanted to better understand and enhance their practice in order to better support their mentees. We also observed that effective teachers and effective mentors share a disposition that includes the following elements:

- *Honest Self-Reflection*: A mentor has greater experience in the field, yet has not forgotten that much of that experience has been gained from mistakes made and learning accumulated over time.
- *Openness to Listening and Sharing*: A mentor is a strong listener who takes time to appreciate with an open mind the cultural, social, emotional, and economic factors that influence newcomers to the profession, regardless of their age or prior experience.
- *Willingness to Make Professional Practice Public*: A mentor reaches beyond the sharing of knowledge and the demonstration of skills to support a mentee in understanding the thinking processes and the rationale that underpin the responsibilities, actions, and activities a teacher implements in the classroom. In doing so, a mentor deprivatizes and makes visible their practice, even though it may mean exposing their own vulnerability.

See Chapter 3 for more on reciprocal learning.

- *Recognition of the Value of Reciprocal and Active Learning*: A mentor is a willing learner who understands that a person inexperienced in the field of education brings skills and talents from which both the mentor and the students in the classroom can learn, and that learning is internalized through active engagement and meaningful feedback, rather than from passive observation and critical judgment.

See Chapter 5 for more on creating a mentoring community.

- *Collaboration within Professional Communities:* A mentor is a partner in teaching and learning who inspires, motivates, counsels, and guides to allow a mentee to develop their independence, experience, knowledge, and skills in a safe, inclusive, welcoming, and supportive environment.

The concept of the mentoring role as one of partnership, particularly with a newcomer to the profession, may seem discordant at first. Partnerships generally mean equity in a relationship, and an experienced mentor may seem to bring more to the table in terms of pedagogy and understandings. A mentor who is able to honestly self-reflect will come to see that professional growth and development flows naturally from a mentoring situation. Mentees also have much to share to enrich the partnership.

Stories from the Field: The Tuesday Teacher (Diane and Lana)

In a recent conversation we had with a group of experienced mentor teachers, a teacher commented that she tried to be the best teacher possible on Tuesdays. Tuesday, she went on to explain, was the day of the week when her mentee, a teacher candidate at a local education faculty, spent the day in her classroom. The mentor teacher told us that on Monday evenings she would take extra care to prepare for the next day by organizing her materials, cleaning her classroom, and preparing all her resources in neat piles on her desk. She worked hard on Tuesdays to exemplify being the "best teacher," assuming a persona of perfection so that her mentor didn't see her making any mistakes.

This story opened an avenue of discussion about many varied aspects of mentoring: the myth that we have to be perfect or on point all the time; the vulnerability involved in opening our inner selves, our spaces, and our practices to scrutiny; and the gap between what we believe is expected of us and what our mentees actually want to learn. But underlying all of these issue lies the crux of mentoring: that there must be a relationship between the two (or more) parties involved for there to be any kind of authentic learning or growth.

In essence, the role of the mentor is to offer an invitation to an inclusive, safe, and welcoming physical and intellectual space within which both mentor and mentee can thrive and explore creative new ways to enhance their practice and develop their teaching excellence together. To become comfortable in the role of mentor, it is helpful to begin by getting to know the mentee as an individual with unique qualities, interests, and experiences that can enhance learning for everyone in the classroom (mentor, mentee, and students).

Mentoring Move: Making Connections

Connecting Is Key

"The most important thing I learned is that the mentor/mentee relationship is a collaboration."
— Mentor Teacher, 2017

- Making connections facilitates relationship-building by creating a space for educators to share the experiences, histories, perspectives, and pathways that brought both mentor and mentee to teaching.
- Using a storytelling model, mentors and mentees establish and look for commonalities related to experience and history. These commonalities highlight shared experiences and perspectives even when backgrounds, age, and experience differ greatly.
- In a society that honors diversity, the celebration of difference might mask a myriad of commonalities that individuals share. The relationship-building process asks mentors and mentees to look beyond their differences to seek common histories, perspectives, and aspirations they share.

3 Simple Steps

1. Mentors and mentees use the sentence starters in the Making Connections narrative template (see page 29) to share their teaching and learning stories. The objective is to find as many commonalities as possible. A broad opening can be refined to highlight common experiences. For example, the starter *I was born...* might result in a common finding such as *...the eldest in my family, ...to immigrant parents, ...thousands of kilometres from where we sit today*, or *...in the heart of a city.*
2. With a focus on similarities rather than differences, mentors and mentees seek ways they are connected to each other through shared experience. As they do so, the story becomes one story that reflects the common experiences of both. Using the Making Connections template on page 29 to make a cube, mentors and mentees write one common experience on each of the six faces of the cube.

See page 29 for the Making Connections template.

3. After making several connections, the stories end with a glimpse into the future. Mentors and mentees share common aspirations that can include career objectives, learning goals, travel dreams, or shared visions of education, teaching, or other related issues, and they examine shared goals.

Next Steps

- Focus on the common aspirations you share to move beyond the differences of the moment. Use the identified commonalities to celebrate connection. Acknowledge differences in ways of thinking or undertaking practice to mitigate challenges to the relationship and to highlight both commonalities and diversity as a strength of the partnership.
- Reinforce the connections between mentor and mentee through social conversation to relieve the stress of a busy day or challenging workplace situation. For example, two tea drinkers might share a cup of fine tea during a break, or two music lovers might enjoy some background music playing as they wind down the day.
- Focus on connections to strengthen the mentor/mentee relationship.

What does the process of mentoring look like?

The Mentoring Process

The mentoring process will differ as much as the individuals who engage with it. However, there are fundamental objectives that the process sets out to achieve. While the route to arrive at the objectives may vary, the final outcome of the mentoring experience should provide both mentor and mentee with a sense of shared accomplishment in having achieved these overall mentoring objectives:

- Development of a professional demeanor appropriate to the environment that reflects the requirements of the faculty/school district/governing body.
- Development of skills to enhance ongoing professional communication, collaboration, engagement, and learning.
- Development of an understanding of learners, the learning environment, and the community.
- Development of knowledge, skills, and strategies relative to the field.

See Chapter 2 for more on knowledge and skills development.

Professional Demeanor

Stories from the Field: Wearing your Profession (Diane)

In my work with a large urban faculty of education, I am often required to support preservice teachers who are struggling in their practice. For those who have challenges with what I classify as the technical aspects of teaching (lesson planning, assessment, organization), I have strategies to share and resources to recommend to facilitate stronger practice.

A much more difficult issue to address is professionalism or, more specifically, the lack thereof. For preservice teachers who have yet to develop a fulsome understanding of what it means to be a professional educator, the theoretical understandings that they bring from university coursework are often overlooked. Particularly during times of stress, reactions to classroom situations or interpersonal issues in the placement can result in inappropriate or unprofessional responses. Such incidents generally cause greater concern for mentors and schools. While a misstep in lesson-planning might simply indicate a need for more experience, a misstep in professionalism often affects the future of the mentoring partnership.

A colleague once suggested that preservice teachers focus on maintaining their professional demeanor by "wearing" their profession. For some, consistent visualization of themselves as professional educators was a sufficient reminder to maintain a professional demeanor. For others, this might mean physically dressing in a manner that reminds them of their role as professionals, or working with a heightened sense of awareness of how they are representing themselves in manner and communication within the school environment.

Some preservice or novice teachers have found it helpful to think of donning their professional cloak as they cross the threshold into the school. A visualized professional cloak does not hide the authentic person; it allows a newcomer to the profession to access to the role of teacher as they internalize the manner of communication, ethical standards, and ways of being that are expected, and often legislated, within the professional environment. It is not about presenting yourself as something you are not. Rather, it is a means to try on a role as you adjust the fit and become more comfortable in the environment.

Another strategy we use is asking mentees to think of the teacher who inspired them when they were students. How would they describe that teacher? How might they become that teacher for a student in their host classroom? What specific aspects of that inspiring teacher's demeanor might they bring to their own work? What would a mentee expect of a teacher responsible for the education of their child, younger sibling, or family member? Mentors are advised to do likewise. How did their mentor inspire and enhance their practice? How are they actively inspiring and enhancing the practice of their mentee?

The reality is that newcomers to the profession will make missteps as they gain professional understandings. As guide and counsellor, the mentor needs to support a mentee through sharing their experience, maintaining a nonjudgmental stance and facilitating supported decision-making that calls on the mentee to think through issues and the implications of teacher response.

Communication Skills

Teaching is all about relationships. We maintain relationships with students, parents, colleagues, administration, teaching federations, policy makers, and the community surrounding the school. One of the pillars of any relationship is effective communication. In an age when social media and online representation can instantly damage reputations, it is of particular importance that mentors and mentees think within and beyond the classroom when considering how professional communication affects relationships.

No doubt, everyone has heard horror stories about Internet posts going viral. A derogatory passing remark overheard in the hallway or other public place can do as much damage.

Stories from the Field: Rewind (Diane)

I recall ....

- A mentee who shared a coffee with her mentor in a local café at the end of the day. As she complained about a student who had challenged her all day, she didn't realize the father of the student was sitting at an adjacent table.
- A novice male teacher who accepted a Facebook friend request from a female student. The student boasted to classmates about her new Facebook friend and shared the social posts and comments the teacher had made on his page. It soon got back to parents, who felt the teacher's action required his removal from the school.
- A student teacher whose reply to a faculty advisor's email included a litany of complaints about her mentor, not realizing that her mentor had been copied on the original message and, therefore, on the reply.

We often use the toothpaste analogy when talking about professional communication: Once it is out of the tube, it is impossible to get it back in again. Maintaining a professional stance in all types of communication (face-to-face, written, or electronic) avoids much potential embarrassment, offence, and conflict. Open and nonjudgmental conversations about professional communication and communication protocols will avoid most concerns. The following tips will help mentors and mentees:

- Remember that a mentoring relationship is professional. That does not mean that it cannot be friendly; however, an awareness of the professional nature of the relationship should always be recognized.
- Use a workplace or university email address for all online communication, with consideration of the fact that any communication may potentially become public.
- Schedule a time and private professional space for confidential or challenging conversations. Library seminar rooms or other workspaces often allow for private conversation.
- Talk about evidence (what you have observed) and its impact on students, learning, and the classroom environment, avoiding accusations, unconstructive comments, or flippant remarks that might be misperceived.
- Check out these Mentoring Moves to shift from evaluative feedback to supported- and self-assessment: Targeted Feedback (page 47); Stoplight Self-Assessment (page 50); Scaling Questions (page 96).

Understanding Learners

One of our primary objectives as teachers must be to understand the learners with whom we work, the environment within which we are working, and the community that influences both the learners and the environment. Without these understandings, we are simply delivering content that may or may not be relevant, may or may not be engaging, and/or may or may not be valuable to our learners.

Stories from the Field: Make Yourself at Home (Diane)

When I welcome a mentee into our environment, it is important to me to help them feel at home. As a classroom teacher, I spend a lot of time and energy each fall making my classroom a welcoming space. The beginning of a new academic year generally includes ice-breaking activities, establishment of classroom relationships and routines, and creation of a physical space that reflects the faces of our students. Many of us dedicate the first few weeks of a new academic year to prioritizing the creation of a classroom community because we know that learning is greater when students take ownership of the space, the community, and, subsequently, the learning. The importance of developing an understanding of the learners, the learning environment, and the greater community is equally important for newcomers to the teaching profession. I believe that a focus on developing these understandings at the beginning of a mentoring relationship will lay a foundation for future success. Mentoring a new colleague or preservice teacher may not coincide neatly with the beginning of an academic year. A newcomer to the profession might be arriving to fill a leave of absence or for a preservice practicum experience. Re-creating that first-few-weeks-of-school experience mid-term may not be practical. However, simple activities can provide opportunities for mentor, mentee, and students in the classroom to get to know each other at any time of year.

Mentoring Move: Jumpstart the Relationship

Integration Is Key

"After having time to talk with (my mentee) today, I rethought the way I would be with a (mentee) next year."
— Mentor Teacher, 2017

- Mentees beginning a relationship mid-term often feel like outsiders in the well-established relationship between the mentor and the students.
- Time is rarely available for the kind of relationship-building activities that are often undertaken at the beginning of an academic year.
- Integrated activities that engage the mentee and students in curriculum-related conversation can facilitate getting to know each other and help to jumpstart the relationship between mentee, mentor, and students in the classroom.

3 Simple Steps

See page 30 for the Jumpstart the Relationship template.

1. Mentor, mentee, and students use the sentence starters from the chart in the Jumpstart the Relationship template on page 30 to identify themselves relative to the age-level and curriculum content. For example: *If I were a historical figure, I would be...* This can also be used as a group activity, with the group agreeing on an animal that represents them all. For example: *Our group chooses a rabbit to represent the group, because W is always on the go, X is a vegetarian, Y is quiet, and Z is a good listener.*

2. Respondents support their choice with rationale, which helps the newcomer/mentee gain insights into each respondent's personality or characteristics.
3. Depending on time available, whole-class sharing can take place via face-to-face discussion, a bulletin-board post, or an internal class web post.

Next Steps

- Encourage the mentee to recognize what the responses reveal. The student who identifies as a giraffe (because they are quiet) may reveal to a classroom newcomer that the student feels intimidated if called on to answer a question in front of the class.
- Encourage the mentee to use a student's "I would be..." choice as a conversation opener. For example, they could ask "Have you read...?", "Did you know...?", or "I wonder..." in keeping with the student's interest.

Active Engagement

For more information, please see Chapter 2 for focused conversation related to Knowledge and Skills, including the following Mentoring Moves:

- Articulation to Action (page 38)
- Thinking Aloud (page 44)
- Co-acting for Learning (page 41)
- Targeted Feedback (page 47)
- Stoplight Self-Assessment (page 50)
- Needs Analysis (page 52)

Our overall experience in working with mentors has clearly shown us that knowledge, skills, and strategies develop gradually over time, supported by many opportunities for active engagement by the mentee in the daily practice of the classroom. While observation may happen concurrently, active engagement is key to the internalization or acquisition (Gee, 2008) of learning. Facilitating active engagement in the classroom can be challenging in certain situations. Teachers ask, "What does active engagement look like in the classroom?" and "How can I provide feedback to a mentee if we are both immersed in the work of the classroom at the same time?" We discuss these important questions in detail in Chapter 2.

How does mentoring differ from modelling best practice?

Mentoring vs Modelling

Teaching is a profession of caring and nurturing. Teachers want to give their very best to the students in their classrooms. Since mentoring is a responsive process that sees the learner as an individual, the goal of mentoring is to facilitate the mentee's development of their best professional self. A mentor values the strengths of the mentee and respects the mentee's individuality as they develop understandings and gain experience in the profession.

Stories from the Field: Modelled Practice (Diane)

I recall joining a new school to teach Grade 1. After having set up literacy circles, putting up an environmental print wall, and teaching reading strategies (Fountas & Pinnell, 2001), I was delighted with the progress my students were making. One day after school, a colleague with 25 years of experience came to the classroom to express concern that I permitted the students to sit in groups and talk. The colleague then modelled the practice she had used for those 25 years, which included writing fill-in-the-blank sentences on the board. A series of magnetic drawings (ball, book, cat, dog, etc.) were then inserted in the blank spaces and a pointer was used to tap the blackboard at each word so that students could read in unison. To engage non-participating students, my colleague suggested that I tap the pointer more firmly and loudly on the board to get students' attention.

A few days later, the colleague returned to my classroom to remark that when she looked in my door, she had noticed that I did not seem to be following the modelled practice. I suggested that perhaps we had two different philosophies of teaching literacy and might agree to disagree on best practice; however, the colleague was upset that her model had not been adopted in my classroom.

This example from personal experience highlights the objective of modelling, rather than mentoring. Modelling generally has an expert demonstrate best practice and a learner copy or mimic the practice. Through modelling, a learner becomes indoctrinated into a club of others who think alike and follow like practices. Modelling is a form of direct instruction that leaves little room for independent thinking on the part of the learner or for consideration of alternative ways of doing, being, or knowing. Modelling is not responsive to the specific needs of the learner; rather, it demands that the learner adopt the method as demonstrated by the expert. The expert provides the model and the newcomer internalizes it, then performs by following the same pattern and practice. In doing so, the learner becomes a replica of the model.

To provide an example of how modelling and mentoring differ in practical application, the following sample conversation demonstrates the two approaches.

Grade 7 Literacy Block

Modelling	**Mentoring**
Mentor: *I noticed that Group A is struggling with the text. They don't seem to be grasping the author's meaning. I don't think they are making connections between the text and their own experience or other similar texts.* *Today I would like you to sit with that group and talk to them about the importance of making text-to-self and text-to-text connections to improve meaning making.* *Here is an activity with prompts that you can use with the group during our Literacy Block. Following the lesson, we can look at the activity sheets to evaluate if the students have bettered their meaning making skills.*	Mentor: *I read an interesting article about enhancing meaning-making for adolescent readers. I would be happy to share it with you. I have observed that Group A needs support.* Mentee: *We discussed meaning-making in a literacy course I took. Our course director gave us an interesting article about developing metacognition to help adolescent readers make meaning of text.* Mentor: *That sounds very interesting. Perhaps we could swap articles, then discuss the best way to help students in Group A. They really seem to be struggling and it would be great to collaborate to find creative ways to support them.*

Having mentored teachers at all stages of their careers, we understand the busy-ness that mentoring while teaching can create. Initially, it might seem easier to simply act as a model, providing support and direct instruction to the mentee. However, if you set the precedent of modelling early in the mentoring relationship, it can result in mentees expecting to be handed what they need throughout the mentoring period. The danger is that the mentee becomes dependent on the mentor to provide lesson plans, activities, and/or solutions to classroom concerns and is thereby reluctant to take ownership of or responsibility for the learning.

There is an old adage: Start the way you mean to finish. While we would agree that this is sage advice in all aspects of life, it is particularly apt when talking about mentoring. It is important that, at the beginning of the relationship, you make clear that collaboration, creativity, and responsibility are mutual expectations within a mentoring relationship.

See Chapter 2 for Mentoring Move: Thinking Aloud.

A mentee who is less eager to demonstrate independence at the beginning of a mentoring relationship may need support in gaining confidence. Undertaking a task, planning a lesson, or thinking for a mentee will not support confidence-building. If you share responsibility for a task, collaborate in lesson planning, and think aloud through a pedagogical process, it will allow a mentee to engage actively with the work of the classroom while gaining confidence in their own abilities.

Modelling practice on an ongoing basis becomes a chore. Mentoring is an action of professional development shared between mentor and mentee; consequently, mentoring is a process that supports the professional growth and development of the mentor and the mentee without adding significantly to the mentor's daily workload. A true mentoring relationship is mutually beneficial to the mentor and the mentee, and also to students in the classroom, whose learning is enhanced by the presence of two collaborating professionals.

Mentoring Move: Model to Mentor

Mentoring Is Key

"We are all constantly learning, not just imparting knowledge based on our experiences."
— Mentor Teacher, 2017

- A mentor creates an open and inclusive environment that encourages a mentee to demonstrate the best of their professional self, to take calculated risks in practice in order to develop a comfort level in the profession, and to become the professional they aspire to be.
- The objective of mentoring is *not* to create a clone of the mentor nor to inculcate a novice.
- To move from model to true mentor, it is important to set aside preoccupations with the way it has always been done and to honor the intentions, and the professional decisions and aspirations, of the mentee as an empowered critical thinker and educator.

3 Simple Steps

1. Mentor and mentee discuss the learning outcomes of a proposed lesson/unit to brainstorm novel, out-of-the-box thinking and alternative instructional strategies.
2. Using a lesson study model, mentor and mentee collaborate as participant observers to develop, implement, and observe all aspects of the lesson and the learners. Following the lesson, artifacts of learning or student work are brought to the discussion.
3. Based on prompts from the Model to Mentor template on page 31, mentor and mentee engage in collaborative analysis of the lesson, using observations of artifacts collected as evidence of student learning. Mentor and mentee highlight specific strengths and challenges of the lesson, aspects of the lesson that worked or did not work for their personal teaching styles, and suggestions of how they might change the lesson for future implementation.

See page 31 for the Model to Mentor template.

Next Steps

- Collaboratively develop a teaching strategy that might address concerns or support student needs as highlighted by evidence from the lesson observation.
- Engage students in providing feedback about how the lesson affected their learning.

- In collaboration with other mentors and mentees, undertake the process of assessing how the learning outcomes for students vary due to factors of classroom dynamic.
- Write up the findings of the lesson study to share with colleagues at a staff meeting or on a blog.

What attributes best support the role of mentor?

Attributes of a Mentor

The attributes of an exemplary teacher are those of a strong mentor. They may not be skills that are generally taught, but they are qualities that can be developed through honest and conscious self-reflection. A mentor who is able to honestly self-reflect will be able to empathize and show compassion for a struggling mentee, or watch as a stellar mentee takes flight to innovate or initiate new ideas that the mentor has yet to ponder.

Stories from the Field: What Makes a Great Teacher? (Diane)

When I meet teacher candidates for the first time, I ask them to share adjectives that describe a teacher who has motivated them to join the profession. These words describe the character and the ethical essence of a teacher. They also paint a picture of teachers who share their passion for learning and for their subject, rather than those who simply know their subject well. This word graphic displays the most common adjectives used.

When we have compiled the list, I read it back to teacher candidates and tell them that they have demonstrated that they know exactly what it takes to be an exemplary teacher. I tell them that, beyond those attributes, which we trust they have brought with them to the profession, we will be happy to add theoretical learning and practical professional experience to ensure that they become that exemplary teacher who motivates and inspires students in their future classrooms.

To apply concrete understandings to adjectives that might seem to be abstract, we have created some questions that teachers who are ready to become mentors may wish to consider.

How do I react to challenging situations?

Effective mentors are problem-solvers who are willing to address challenging situations in a calm and organized manner. They seek ways to communicate and dismantle roadblocks to continue on the journey. They are open-minded to new ideas and new ways of thinking, being, and knowing. They see constructive criticism as a tool for professional growth.

Am I open to collaboration with colleagues?

Effective mentors are keen collaborators who understand that stronger teaching in all classrooms enhances student learning and reflects well on the entire school community. They share resources, ideas, and experiences to the benefit of all. They are motivated by collective excellence.

Is my classroom door usually open or closed?

Effective mentors are willing to deprivatize their practice. They are confident that the work they are doing in the classroom is worthy of sharing, even when the calculated risks they take with their pedagogy fail to yield the anticipated results.

Do I engage willingly with professional learning opportunities?

Effective mentors would rather seek new opportunities to learn than rush to defend historical ways of teaching. They value of professional growth with the understanding that knowledge, like water, needs to shift and flow to avoid stagnation.

When faced with negativity, how do I choose to react?

Effective mentors refuse to turn to judgment when considering the actions or reactions of others. They attempt to understand what motivates the behavior. They also reflect on what story is told by their personal reaction in a given situation, asking themselves, "What did I feel in that situation and why?"

What type of relationship do I have with my students?

Effective mentors recognize that they are human. They recognize mistakes or misspeakings that challenge relationships and set aside pride to mend them. If you asked students in your classroom to describe you with character adjectives, what would they say? What might you do differently moving forward?

What does the physical environment of my classroom say to an outsider?

Effective mentors create a physical space that reflects the students in their classroom and their philosophy of teaching and learning. The space is invitational, inclusive, and in harmony with the objectives of the learning.

What does my school involvement look like beyond my classroom?

Effective mentors respect the fact that lives and families demand attention at the end of the working day. They set realistic expectations for themselves and invite their mentees to do likewise. They understand that what is possible for one teacher might not be possible for others, due to personal, family, or economic circumstances. Occasional or preservice teachers might be holding down an evening or weekend job to adequately support their families as they pursue their dream to teach. All teachers may be juggling faculty coursework or additional qualifications.

What do I know about the community surrounding my school?

Effective mentors understand that the school does not exist in a vacuum. The community grounds the school and imposes certain values on the work. The realities of life in the community put demands on students, whether that be high academic or athletic achievement, economic strain, social pressures, or other responsibilities. Effective mentors know the community well. They encourage mentees to do likewise by taking a community walk or participating in a community event so that they might see their students in a different setting.

As teachers, all of us bring specific strengths and challenges to our work in schools. To suggest that there is a specific skill set that all mentors possess would be misleading. Nevertheless, in our experience, effective mentors are

- Well-organized in their practice: Mentees are generally looking for key strategies to get them off on the right foot. A mentor's organizational strategies might not suit the mentee's personality; however, the value of organization when entering a world that can seem overwhelming and chaotic cannot be overstated.
- Knowledgeable in their subject, grade, or division: Inviting a mentee into the classroom when the mentor is becoming acclimated to a new subject, grade, or division can put undue stress on both mentor and mentee. If it is a new grade, subject, or division for the mentor, there should be an immediate openness about the learning journey that will be shared.
- Capable of engaging their students in learning: Mentees need a stable and consistent environment in which to develop their teaching skills. Mentees need to see the impact of engagement on learning. A stable and consistent learning environment allows mentees to pursue their learning objectives without fear that chaos will ensue if there is a break from daily routine or if a lesson fails to hit the mark.

Positivity

We have all heard the saying, "They will forget what you said—but they will never forget how you made them feel" (Buehner, in Evans, 1971). Mentors need to ensure that their mentees feel they can succeed. Certainly, mentees will make mistakes; we all do. However, the frustration of feeling that it is impossible to succeed can be soul-destroying. Many preservice or novice teachers over the years who have floundered in a mentoring situation that made them feel incompetent in the profession have gone on to soar to great achievement when placed with a mentor who believed in them and demonstrated the positivity that made the mentee feel that success was within reach.

Mentoring Move: Positivity as Practice

Positivity Is Key

"I feel like I'm walking away with a plan and goals. I feel like I have an opportunity to improve."
—Teacher Candidate, 2017

- Positivity requires a mindset that focuses on enhancing practice through a positive stance. In contrast to a deficit or corrective mindset that seeks to identify and correct errors, positivity positions mentors and mentees as inquiry-based learners seeking ways to improve both the mentoring relationship and classroom practice.

- Mentors and mentees will explore their understandings and the impact of positive feedback to enhance the mentoring relationship and as a form of inquiry-based professional development.
- Positivity as practice does not deny mistakes or challenges; rather, it chooses to acknowledge them as realities of learning, and then cast them in a light of positive challenge and opportunity for growth.

3 Simple Steps

1. Seek evidence of learning (or nonlearning) in student work through assessment, then use the evidence to provide feedback to the mentee on lesson implementation. Brainstorm ways that teaching practice might be adapted to support stronger results in student understanding. For example:

> Mentor: "I noticed that the students were not able to complete the task independently, although they were doing so with your help."
>
> Mentee: "Maybe I should have asked more questions so I had a better feel for their level of understanding before moving on to independent practice."

See page 32 for the Positivity as Practice template.

2. Use Questions and Prompts from the Positivity as Practice template on page 32 to discuss the types of feedback that were most helpful, how using evidence of student learning could improve practice, and how applying feedback could result in change. For example:

> Mentee: "I found it really helpful when you provided evidence of where the breakdown in learning occurred. It allowed me to realize that I need to develop my questioning skills to better understand where students are in their learning during a lesson."

3. End with affirmations of the learning from the process. State concrete changes to practice that will be implemented as a result of the conversation and record on the chart on the Positivity as Practice template on page 32. For example:

> Mentor: *I will make a conscious effort to share my observations about student learning to help you think of ways to improve your planning.*
>
> Mentee: *I will prepare higher-level probing questions for students so I can better understand where they are during guided practice.*

Next Steps

- Consider specific objectives for future inquiry to support the enhancement of practice; e.g. readings, research, inquiry conversations with colleagues.
- Continue to work with evidence from student work to support professional learning conversations.
- On an ongoing basis, think about how the tone and language of a message you communicate is being heard by the listener. Does it sound judgmental instead of being a genuine demonstration of support or inquiry? Does it respect the other within the professional mentor/mentee relationship?

How might we build trust in a mentoring relationship?

Building Trust

In their research, Bryk and Schneider (2003) concluded, "Relational trust is the connective tissue that binds individuals together to advance the education and welfare of students." They found that the most successful schools showed evidence of strong relations between teachers, while the least successful schools were marked by poor relations between teachers. Within a relationship founded on trust, there is much opportunity for self-expression and creativity because the other has confidence that their partner is acting at all times in good faith. When challenges present themselves, the foundation of trust allows for mistakes to be accepted as part of the learning experience and assurance that there was no ill intent. Bryk and Schneider (2003) identify four elements that are critical to establishing trust: respect, personal regard, competence in core role responsibilities, and personal integrity.

Respect

Respect is defined as genuine listening and valuing opinions of others. We define genuine listening as listening between the lines.

Stories from the Field: Say What You Mean (Diane)

I recall a mentee who asked a mentor to take a quick look at a lesson. The mentor spent a great deal of time reviewing the lesson and shared detailed suggestions, each of them prefaced by a polite phrase, such as "You might want to think about..." or "If you wanted to, you could..." The mentee, after thinking about the suggestions, decided not to implement the changes, as acting on them would have entailed significant changes in the lesson for which there was little time.

The mentor was disturbed that the advice had not been taken. In hindsight, it was clear that neither had listened between the lines. The mentee had asked for a "quick look" rather than a reconstruction of the lesson. The mentor had phrased the suggestions in such as manner that the mentee took them as good suggestions for future planning, but not changes required to meet the objective of the lesson. Therefore, the mentee presumed it was fine to go ahead without implementing the suggestions. The miscommunication was eventually resolved but could have been avoided with more careful listening.

Personal Regard

Personal regard reflects a willingness to extend beyond formal roles and an effort to reduce others' sense of vulnerability. In the mentoring context, this reflects our original Oxford definition of mentoring as going "beyond mere teaching or tutoring to include advice and guidance about many other issues and problems encountered by students." A mentor's role does not begin and end with modelling a lesson, activity, or practice. A mentor offers support, which includes guidance and advice about professional standards and ethical concerns, classroom relationships, and management; open communication with all of the stakeholders involved in the learning; and more.

Competence

Competence is the ability to execute one's responsibilities and the recognition of the interdependence of roles in attaining objectives. In the mentoring context this means

- Making the time to discuss matters of importance to the mentor or mentee
- Meeting deadlines for tasks or activities
- Accepting ownership of and responsibility for their part in supporting student learning
- Providing feedback in a timely manner (to each other and to students in the classroom)
- Creating a safe, respectful, and inclusive classroom environment

Personal Integrity

Finally, personal integrity is demonstrated through consistency between what one says and what one does. This means that a mentor and mentee must be able to rely on each other to meet commitments, to behave in a manner consistent with the values that they share as professional educators, and to demonstrate dedication to achieving the shared objectives.

Mentoring Move: Relational Trust

Trust Is Key

"Mentoring is really important. When I face new challenges, I like to build that relationship with someone who's been there before. So, I wanted to do that with them [mentees]."
— Mentor Teacher, 2017

- Relational Trust (Bryk & Schneider, 2003) has been identified as a major factor in advancing education in schools. Building trust takes time but trust can be quickly undermined by inattention or careless action.
- This Mentoring Move helps mentors and mentees establish an understanding of the core elements of trust and builds awareness of the importance of maintaining that trust in a strong professional relationship.

3 Simple Steps

See page 33 for the Relational Trust template.

While this Mentoring Move can be used at any time, implementation is recommended subsequent to Mentoring Move: Making Connections, which builds a foundational relationship upon which this move can be launched.

1. Mentors and mentees review the key elements of trust as outlined on pages 23–24: respect, personal regard, competence in core role responsibilities, and integrity.
2. Dedicated time is set aside to examine each key element and to collaboratively determine what each element looks like in practice within the specific work environment. Using prompts from the Relational Trust template on page 33, mentors and mentees identify the specifics of what relational trust means within the mentoring relationship.
3. End with the creation of a brief joint commitment statement. This statement will take the format of *The Mentor will...* and *The Mentee will...*, and will take into consideration the specific requirements of the environment, the identified competencies, and the needs of both mentor and mentee.

The Next Steps

- Print out a copy of the joint commitment statement as a reminder of the importance of maintaining the trust.
- Use the key elements of trust as the standard against which you measure the appropriateness of your responses or reactions to conflicts or issues that arise in the teaching environment. Ask yourself if your response enhances or erodes relational trust.

- Presume only the best intentions of your mentor or mentee. Remember that a sharp word or a tired look your way may have nothing to do with you; rather, it might reflect a response to factors beyond the classroom.

What do mentees expect of their mentors?

Clarifying Expectations

Dissatisfaction in relationships often results when prior expectations are not met. During schoolboard workshops with mentors and their mentees, we asked mentees what they were looking for in a mentor. The following table provides their responses, further details that we retrieved from comments during the session, and the Mentoring Moves we developed in response to the comments of both mentors and mentees in our research.

Mentee Response	Clarification	Mentoring Moves
Make time for us	Mentees understand that a school day is busy; nevertheless, they know that setting aside time to talk is critical to their learning.	Walk 'n' Talk (page 27) Targeted Feedback (page 47)
Be open to our ideas	Mentees have much to contribute to the classroom. Many have had significant prior experience working with students in a number of capacities. Their skills and talents can enhance classroom learning.	What I Bring (page 63)
Let us flop and be supportive when we do	We all learn from experience, including unsuccessful experiences. Mentees appreciate the opportunity to take calculated pedagogical risks. They seek a mentor in whom they can confide their concerns about practice without censure or judgment.	Positivity as Practice (page 21) Relational Trust (page 24)
Display emotional intelligence	Mentees appreciate mentors who are empathetic to the challenges they face.	Making Connections (page 11) Relational Trust (page 24)
Explain the *whys* of your practice	Mentees may be able to see what you are doing and how you are doing it, but why you use specific strategies or the rationale for choices of resources might not always be clear.	Articulation to Action (page 38) Thinking Aloud (page 44) Opening Up Practice (page 88)

Be reflective	Mentees want to know the human side of the role of a teacher and how mentors have come to develop their practice.	Making Connections (page 11) Storytelling (page 116) Sharing Values (page 65)
Be supportive	Mentees want to feel that a mentor will guide and support them as they plan lessons and interact with students in the classroom, while also facilitating their independence.	Co-acting for Learning (page 41)
Be equity-minded	Mentees are keen to feel welcome in a safe and inclusive classroom environment.	A Space for Open Minds (page 90) A Critical Lens (page 98)
Give in-depth feedback	Mentees are eager to hear constructive feedback on their work. Saying that a lesson was "good" does not provide the specifics that they need to improve.	Stoplight Self-Assessment (page 40) Scaling Questions (page 96) Targeted Feedback (page 47)
Lead by example	Leading by example is not about modelling practice; rather, it is about demonstrating integrity and competence.	Relational Trust (page 24) Tomorrow's Leaders (page 100) Model to Mentor (page 18)
Adapt to new technologies and practices	Mentees are seeking a mentor who is willing to be a co-learner in exploring new ideas and pedagogies.	Inquiring Collaboratively (page 76) Wondering (page 93)
Be approachable	An approachable mentor is open-minded and in tune to the needs of a mentee.	Needs Analysis (page 52)
Be fun and engaging	Mentees hope to find a mentor in whose company they can be comfortable. They seek a mentor who shares their love of teaching and engages with the mentee in daily practice.	Inquiring Collaboratively (page 76) The Important Thing (page 73)

Be energizing	When acclimating to a new profession, learning new ways of thinking and being can be challenging and exhausting. Mentees who are juggling course work or busy personal lives can find themselves wearied by academic and emotional demands. A mentor keeps the energy level up with positive encouragement to support a mentee in achieving their full potential, and with encouragement to identify and focus on the important issues or skills in that particular moment.	Positivity as Practice (page 21) The Important Thing (page 73)

To help keep everyone on the same page, a shared electronic calendar can be of value. Both mentor and mentee can record upcoming tasks, deadlines, and other expectations. Another handy tool is a shared electronic folder and/or shared classroom basket that might hold lesson plans and reflections, readings or research of mutual interest, to-do lists, and other shared resources. A binder or electronic folder containing documented evidence of the mentoring journey will facilitate discussion about the progress of the mentoring relationship or, if required, assessment or evaluation information for submission to a faculty or governing body.

In the end, what a mentee expects and what a mentor is able to give may perfectly align. If not, it is important to have that conversation sooner rather than later.

Mentoring Move: Walk 'n' Talk

Communication Is Key

"I desperately want to mentor you but don't have much time."
—Mentor Teacher, 2017

Communication between mentor and mentee is the key to building a relationship. When open communication exists, the opportunity to share thoughts, concerns, and celebrations deepens the relationship and supports it when challenges arise. Time is always an issue. Talking while walking can be a great stress reliever and allows for deeper reflection and more open sharing when eye-to-eye contact is replaced by a shoulder-to-shoulder proximity.

3 Simple Steps

See page 34 for the Walk 'n' Talk template.

1. Find time during lunch or recess to reduce stress, improve wellness, and communicate openly by taking a brief walk together. Allow the Walk 'n' Talk experience to become a get-away from the fast pace of the school day.
2. Use questions like the ones on the Walk 'n' Talk template on page 34 to strengthen the relationship. While there may be times when pressing pedagogical matters dominate the conversation, this time is best used for mentor and mentee to get to know each other better. Take time to share glimpses into individual aspirations and expectations for the mentoring time together.

3. Ensure that the Walk 'n' Talk conversations remain privileged between mentor and mentee. A confidence shared during a Walk 'n' Talk should never be shared beyond the partnership.

Next Steps

- Be patient. Getting to know each other and feeling comfortable enough to speak more openly takes time.
- Once the pathway to sharing has been opened, the Walk 'n' Talk activity can become a catalyst for richer conversations that reach into the classroom environment.
- The Walk 'n' Talk can also become a wonderful brainstorming environment that inspires both mentor and mentee to think outside the box about professional learning or new pedagogies they might want to explore together.

Making Connections

Conversation Starters

- A memory I have from being a student in school:
- One my earliest moments in the classroom highlights…
- What brought me to teaching:
- My first experiences of teaching:
- A powerful role model for me:
- A challenging experience:

Connections Cube

1. Print out a connections cube for mentor and mentee. Fold and tape or glue into a cube.
2. Choose a conversation starter from the list to begin.
3. As you share your stories, explore connections as mentor/mentee. Write a commonality that you share on each face of the cube.
4. Keep the connections cube at your workspace to remind you of the connections you have as professionals when differences in ways of thinking or undertaking practice result in challenges to the relationship.

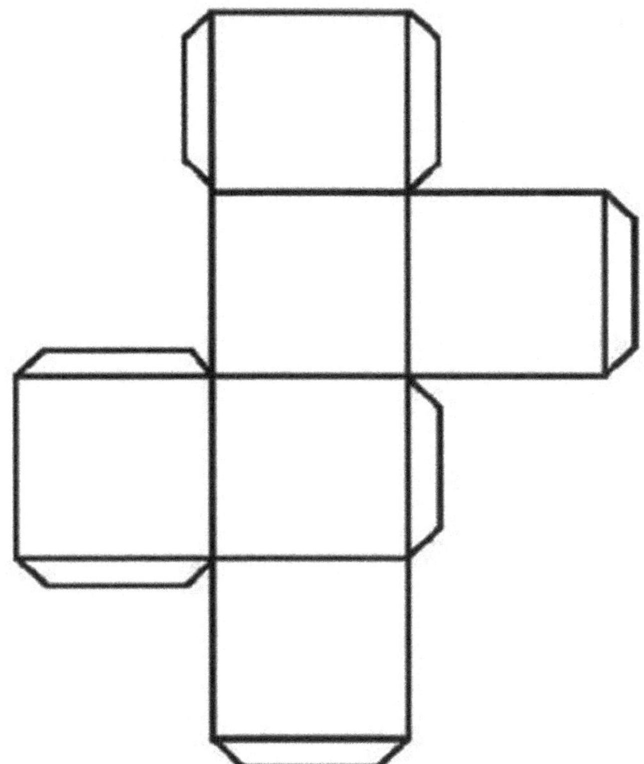

Jumpstart the Relationship

Subject	Sentence Starter	Identification	Reason
Chemistry	If I were a chemical element, I would be...		
English	If I were an author, I would be...		
Geography	If I were a landscape, I would be...		
History	If I were a historical figure, I would be...		
Biology	If I were a plant, I would be...		
Physics	If I were a force, I would be...		
Auto Mechanics	If I were a car, I would be...		
Mathematics	If I were a number, I would be...		
Junior Grade	If I were in a fairy tale, I would be...		
Primary Grade	If I were an animal, I would be...		

Examples of Conversation Openers

- You chose to be number 87 because you are a Crosby fan. What sport do you play?
- You chose to be giraffe because you love to run. Have you read *Giraffes Can't Dance* by Giles Andreae?
- You chose to be a mountain because you love challenges. What is the greatest challenge you have in learning?
- You chose to be a maple tree because you enjoy the change of seasons. What do you do to adapt to changes in the classroom?

Pembroke Publishers ©2020 *Mentoring Each Other* by Lana Parker and Diane Vetter ISBN 978-1-55138-346-0 

Model to Mentor

What was my thought process as I planned this lesson? What did I fail to consider? How did my personal learning styles or ways of thinking have impact on the planning?

How does student work serve as a learning artifact that not only provides evidence of student learning or nonlearning, but also influences my thinking for future planning?

What motivated my choice of resources? How did these choices support or limit learning? What additional resources might be curated in the future?

What did student reactions or behaviors tell me about my instruction or planning? What might future instructional adaptations be?

In what ways did this lesson support the success criteria for my students?

What were some of the challenges for students? How might we support students in thinking about how they learn best to help mitigate these challenges?

What would I do differently next time as part of my pedagogical practice?

Pembroke Publishers ©2020 *Mentoring Each Other* by Lana Parker and Diane Vetter ISBN 978-1-55138-346-0

Positivity as Practice

To be effective, feedback needs to be clear, purposeful, meaningful, and compatible with students' prior knowledge and to provide logical connections. (Hattie & Timperley, p. 104)

Questions and Prompts

- I found it really helpful when…
- I clearly understood when…
- How did you feel when…?
- What did the evidence tell you about…?
- In reimagining ____________, what are your what-if wonderings?
- For me, the most effective part was…
- For me, the greatest challenge was…
- What might learners have been thinking when…?
- How might the physical environment have affected the learning?
- Where might changes make a positive impact?

Mentor: I will…

1.

2.

Mentee: I will …

1.

2.

Mentor and Mentee: We will …

1.

2.

Relational Trust

Respect
Looks like…
Is demonstrated when…
Feels like…
Supports…
Is heard in…

Personal integrity
Looks like…
Is evident when…
Honors…
Reflects…
Models…

Competence in core responsibilities
Looks like…
Includes…
Demonstrates…
Focuses on…
Creates…

Personal regard
Looks like…
Sounds like…
Results in…
Creates…

Joint Commitment Statement

The mentor will

The mentee will

Pembroke Publishers ©2020 *Mentoring Each Other* by Lana Parker and Diane Vetter ISBN 978-1-55138-346-0

Walk 'n' Talk

MENTOR asks…

What was the best part of your day today?

What is one thing you would have liked to do today that didn't happen?

In what ways are your learning expectations being met?

What is one thing we could do differently to better meet your learning expectations?

MENTEE asks…

What improvements did you notice in my practice today?

What is one area of focus that I need to concentrate on to enhance my practice?

In what ways are your expectations for this mentoring experience being met?

What is one thing we could do differently to better meet your expectations of our shared experience?

2

Knowledge and Skills Development

Knowledge and skills development is only one part of the greater mentoring process. As one of the five identified components of effective mentoring, we want to highlight that knowledge and skills development is neither more nor less important than any other component. Rather, it is an equal and vital part of the whole.

When new students arrive at our faculty, they are eager to learn and enthusiastic about heading to practicum. Often we hear student talk about wanting to learn everything there is to know about the teaching process. Indeed, at the beginning it seems there is so much to know and time is of the essence. This chapter will focus on concrete actions to support the development of knowledge and skills in the classroom environment.

Often mentors begin with a prior understanding of mentoring as a process of simply sharing their existing knowledge and skills. Our discussion of knowledge and skills development is based on an understanding that how and what we teach today will be vastly different from how and what we teach in the future. If we consider what teaching looked like not that many years ago in a pre-Internet generation, we can see that classrooms are changing in many ways. Digital environments, classroom technology, and paperless learning are now common. Many of our colleagues are working with *flipped classrooms* (Baker, 2000) that record classroom lectures to be accessed outside the classroom and use class time for student engagement with the learning.

It was not that long ago that we taught our students about nine planets in our solar system; now we teach that there are eight. By the time you read this book, who knows how the knowledge about our solar system may have changed. It is important to recognize that *both* knowledge and desired skills are changing, in both global and local educational contexts. As mentors, we can share our current knowledge and skills, yet always with the understanding that it is important to foster readiness in self-assessing the relevance and accuracy of our knowledge and skills to ensure that we all remain current within a changing education landscape.

To effectively assess changing knowledge and skill requirements, we **articulate our own philosophies** of education and our practice as teachers to enable us to clearly understand the beliefs that underpin our teaching. With a clear understanding of our own thinking, we then explore **co-acting** as a means of sharing what we do in our classrooms. We communicate our existing knowledge and skills by **making visible** to others (mentees and colleagues) the philosophies, thinking, and rationale that ground our practice. As these practices and philosophies unfold in our day-to-day work together, we explore **targeted feedback** to assist both mentor and mentee in assessing the numerous decisions that teachers make throughout a teaching day. Finally, we consider how these conversations naturally provide opportunities for both parties to **self-assess** their practice and knowledge, and how they support collaborative **identification** of mentee needs.

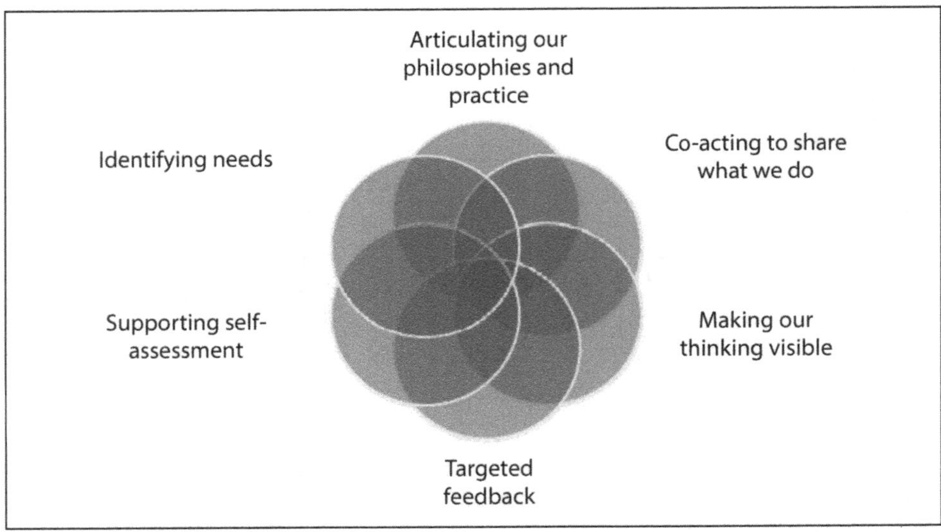

Mentors consider these key questions as they engage with mentees and the mentoring process:

- How might I articulate my philosophies of education and my practice as a teacher? (See page 36.)
- How might I share what I know? (See page 39.)
- How might I make visible to a mentee the thinking and rationale that underpin my teaching? (See page 42.)
- How might I communicate effective feedback on classroom practices and processes? (See page 45.)
- How might I support mentees in self-assessing skills development? (See page 48.)
- How might I help mentees identify their specific needs? (See page 61.)

How might I articulate my philosophies of education and my practice as a teacher?

Articulating Philosophies and Practice

After having spent many years teaching in preservice teacher education, we have observed that "reflection" has become a dreaded word. Teacher candidates groan out loud when asked to reflect yet again on their practice. Nevertheless, we would argue that reflection, when done with intention and purpose, is the finest tool that teachers have to improve how they facilitate learning in the classroom. This is especially true when reflection is implemented as a means of stimulating growth and initiating calculated risk-taking in adopting new pedagogies.

Reflection coupled with action is the difference between a teacher with seven years of experience and a teacher with one year of experience repeated seven times over. Mentors who reflect on their own practice to think beyond *what* they need to teach and *how* they will teach a lesson will come to understand *why* they are teaching a particular way. They are then able to stretch their thinking to envision *what if*—that spark of an idea or vision that moves teaching from good to exemplary.

Stories from the Field: Accidental Discovery (Diane)

It was Friday at lunch and an obstinate photocopy machine was making a teacher's life miserable. She indicated that she was copying a culminating test for social studies in her Grade 7 class that afternoon. When I suggested that she enjoy her lunch and wait until the following week to give the test, she replied "Are you kidding? Those kids won't remember this stuff by next week!"

Once that statement had escaped her mouth, we both laughed at its absurdity. Yet hearing it articulated aloud helped the teacher to recognize that culminating tests of memorized facts were a traditional practice that needed an overhaul. That one articulation of practice led to valuable conversation about alternative ways of assessing student understanding of the meaning and relevance of history, rather than random (forgettable) facts.

Articulation of what, how, and why we undertake specific classroom practices leads us to wonder how often we do things by rote, habit, or tradition in the classroom without thinking deeply about why, questioning if the action is still relevant, wondering how the traditional way affects student learning, or visualizing how our practice might be improved by some out-of-the-box what-if thinking (see Mentoring Move: Opening Up Practice on page 88). We wonder how often we undertake reflection, then lose the impetus to take action within a busy classroom schedule and demanding curriculum, falling back into our comfort zone of traditional ways.

To move from reflection to action, our research and experience indicates that articulating reflections on practice is vital. As Vygotsky (1934/1986) states, "Thought undergoes many changes as it turns into speech. It does not merely find expression in speech; it finds its reality and form" (p. 219). A teacher who articulates reflections with mentees, colleagues, or friends and family generates those "aha!" moments that clarify thinking and motivate action.

Stories from the Field: Talking It Through (Diane)

I noticed that some students in my junior classroom were struggling with writing. As I reflected on my classroom practice, I realized that, as someone who loves literacy, I was using written forms (stories, written responses, text-based projects, etc.) as my main form of assessment. I began wondering how I might change that up. As I talked to a colleague, she said, "Well, you can't eliminate writing from your classroom. What evidence will you have that the kids are achieving the expectations?" That was my "aha!" moment. I realized that the problem was not that kids in my class didn't get it, but that my assessment methods didn't allow all of them to demonstrate it.

In June, when things were slowing down and high temperatures meant short attentions spans, I brainstormed ideas with my colleagues, then declared my class a *pencil-free zone*. We did mental math and math art, oral storytelling, music and poetry presentations, historical dramatizations, and "talk shows" in which students took on various roles to participate in conversations about current issues. In subsequent years, these activities became part of my daily practice, balanced

For a talk show, a group chose to discuss the use of cell phones in classrooms. One student acted as the host, while others played the roles of parent, student, doctor, and cell phone manufacturer, as they presented the perspectives of their characters.

with opportunities for reading and writing. I was amazed to see how the confidence of struggling writers soared through alternative means of demonstrating and articulating their learning.

I also discovered an effective way to collect oral evidence of student learning that I could use for assessment and reporting purposes. I simply divided the number of students in my class by 10, the number of mornings and afternoons in a week. With 28 kids in my class, I made a special point of engaging two or three target students in subtle assessment conversations during a morning or afternoon, while making anecdotal notes. In the end, I had far more evidence of learning than I ever anticipated. I was able to focus on assessing learning across the curriculum, balanced with some specific reading and writing assessments. And I wasn't spending nearly as much time after school grading paper-based assessments.

As a preservice instructor, my favorite assignment now is a formerly text-based memoir of *learning something difficult*. Once I opened it up to multiple modes of expression, I received the most amazing submissions of essays, artwork, dance videos, musical compositions, spoken-word poetry, podcasts, and more. I am consistently impressed by the depth of reflection and the clear articulation of *learning something difficult* that is present in students' work.

Articulating my reflections on my practice has consistently led me to surprising conversations with colleagues, mentees, and family and friends. These conversations have enriched my understandings and my practice, along with student learning in my classroom. In order to articulate your practice and to transform that reflection into meaningful action for change, we suggest a three-step process of reflection, articulation, and action.

Mentoring Move: Articulation to Action

Talking Out Loud Is Key

"It's rare to get opportunity to talk about what we do and how we can do it better, even when I don't have a TC in the classroom."
— Mentor Teacher, 2017

Most of us have had the experience of asking a question about something and having what we don't understand suddenly become clear to us just as we are asking. Research suggests that talking out loud has a direct effect on understanding and problem-solving ability. When we articulate what we know aloud, we are forced to slow down the mental processes and focus on the specifics. As a result, clarity seems to suddenly materialize. In reality, the understanding may have simply been obscured by racing thoughts and lack of focus.

3 Simple Steps

1. Designate one partner as the speaker and the other as the listener. Using a set time (5 to 10 minutes, depending on the availability of time), the speaker articulates their personal philosophies of education, beginning with the phrase, "For me teaching is all about ..." Allow this to be a free flow of ideas rather than a preconstructed monologue. The listener should not interrupt until the allotted time has passed.
2. At the end of the allotted time, the listener asks for clarification of anything that isn't clear, using such questions as "I wasn't sure what you meant when you said..." and "Could you explain a bit more about...?" The speaker responds briefly.
3. It is now the listener's turn. Follow steps 1 and 2 again, allowing the listener to articulate their personal philosophies of education.

Next Steps

- Mentor and mentee take time to analyze the "aha!" moments in their own articulation in order to understand more about the thinking that underpins their teaching practices. Mentor and mentee collaboratively reflect on the articulations and responses to consider where their philosophies converge and where they differ, and then they record on the Articulation to Action template on page 54.
- Mentor and mentee can use the insights into each other's philosophies of education to guide their collaborative practice in the classroom, to understand where differences in planning or pedagogy might arise, and to enact opportunities that respect the philosophies of both mentor and mentee while enhancing both practice and student learning.

See page 54 for the Articulation to Action template.

How might I share what I know?

Co-acting to Share What You Know

Our observation is that, by and large, teachers like to give. Many teachers spend hours outside of the workplace planning, assessing, and worrying about how to give more and do their jobs better. Many spend their own money on supplies for work, looking for ways to ensure that all students can be included; for example, the teacher who miraculously "finds" skates that are a perfect fit for the one kid who otherwise couldn't go to the rink with the rest of the class. In many cases, that giving nature results in a mentor whose initial reaction may be to kindly provide a pile of resources, a list of websites, modelled practice (see Mentoring Move: Model to Mentor on page 18), and an ongoing narrative of tips, advice, information, and indoctrination into the profession. Those of us who have undergone such an experience as a mentee will likely testify to the feelings of being overwhelmed and virtually lost in the well-meaning sharing process. Similarly, many teachers will recall submitting preservice lesson plans that came back with so many sincere suggestions from a host teacher that we didn't know whether to cry or start over from scratch.

Stories from the Field: A Little Too Helpful (Diane)

Jaylen came to speak to me after having experienced challenges in the practicum setting. Mentors and faculty advisors provided significant evidence of ongoing support, so it seemed incongruous that Jaylen continued to struggle so greatly. After a lengthy conversation, it became clear that Jaylen had received so much support that it had become an expectation, and she had a clear lack of initiative to act independently, coupled with a lack of ability to self-assess practice. Jaylen had survived by taking feedback, then implementing a mentor or faculty advisor's recommendations. The issue was certainly one of inability to perform independently; however, it was also an issue of being given such strong support that there was no need for Jaylen to take responsibility for the challenges.

A plan of action to turn around this situation laid responsibility on Jaylen's shoulders to analyze classroom practice through the evidence of student work and engagement (or lack thereof); to identify gaps in knowledge, skills, and strategies; and to determine what might have been done differently to result in a different outcome. When asked to question daily practice, rather than being given answers to the challenges, Jaylen was eventually able to create the independence needed to succeed.

It is a fine line between providing support and enabling dependence. It is also challenging to see a mentee struggle and to see students in the classroom struggle as a result. To avoid having both mentor and mentee feeling lost in the mentoring process, we strongly advocate in favor of the *do with, not for* philosophy that teachers often apply to students (particularly those with exceptionalities) in their classrooms. Engaging *with* a mentee as you plan a lesson, seek out resources, and devise assessments helps the mentor identify which information is most helpful and allows mentees to develop insights into where they are in their learning process and which information, resources, and/or plans are the most valuable in that particular moment. Doing *with* a mentee generally results in conversation, questioning, and active meaning-making on the part of the mentee, with concurrent awareness-building on the part of mentor as to where a mentee is on their learning journey. On the other hand, doing *for* a mentee generally results in the mentor taking the active role and the mentee being a passive listener who is desperately trying to make meaning of the ongoing input.

Engaging *with* a mentee does not mean that mentees never act independently or that mentors need to hover at every moment. Rather, *doing with, not for*, which we call *co-acting*, ensures that mentees feel supported as they engage with the work of the classroom for the entire day. Certainly there may be times when a mentor (or mentee) might take the lead in a lesson or classroom activity, in which case the other is an active observer of what is happening with student learning and engagement. At all times, both partners are consistently engaged in the teaching process.

Mentors and mentees co-act in the classroom when they

- Engage collaboratively with the classroom learning for the entire day. Nobody is sitting on the sidelines. Both partners are actively involved with student learning.
- Collaboratively plan, teach, and assess learning engagements. Unlike team teaching, where teachers divide up tasks and undertake them independently, co-actors are mutually responsible for every aspect of practice.
- Function as two parts of a whole. While one may be leading the learning at a specific moment, the other is always engaged with students, even if that occasionally means working as a participant-observer who provides feedback to their partner on how the learning unfolded for specific students during the lesson.
- Share resources. Many of the mentors we have worked with tell us that one of their motivations for mentoring is to have access to new theories of learning and technologies that preservice or beginning teachers bring to the school.
- Reflect together on the work of the day; share observations of the learning engagement to provide evidence for constructive feedback that facilitates improvements in practice and in student learning. For some partners, this might mean a conversation at the end of each day with a cup of coffee or a walk around the block, an online chat when both have a moment of free time, or a daily check-in to share thoughts and, if necessary, to set up a mutually agreeable time for a more sustained conversation.

Example of Co-acting

Before a Lesson	During a Lesson	After a Lesson
The mentor and mentee meet to discuss the objectives of learning and brainstorm some ideas about how to best facilitate the learning; they work alongside each other to plan, implement, differentiate, sustain, culminate, and assess student learning. The mentor makes visible the thinking and the rationale that supports an effective learning environment for students. (See Making Your Thinking Visible on page 42.)	During the implementation of the lesson, both partners collaborate in supporting student learning, which might mean working with small groups. If a direct instruction approach is used for part of the lesson, then the partner not directing the learning is observing to assess students' reactions and engagement to inform future planning.	The mentor and mentee dedicate time to analyze the lesson in order to share their observations of student learning, to understand successes, to wrestle with challenges, and to consider implications for upcoming plans.

In co-acting, mentor and mentee act as two parts of a whole. Both feel comfortable proposing ideas, making suggestions, and offering feedback. An observer of the lesson should not see an expert and a novice, nor a leader and a follower (for more on deconstructing the hierarchy or power imbalance in a mentoring relationship, see Chapter 3). Rather, the vision should be of partners working with a common purpose toward a common objective; i.e., enhanced student learning.

Mentoring Move: Co-acting for Learning

"We brainstormed, asked questions, learned about growth mindset, and had a chance to evaluate where we are with learning and our relationship."
— Mentor Teacher, 2017

Teamwork Is Key

- Co-acting builds on Vygotsky's theories (1978) that support the concepts of *a zone of proximal development* and *the "more-knowledgeable other"*. In this Mentoring Move, the mentor is the more-knowledgeable other, whose support allows the mentee to work within a zone that lies beyond their immediate reach.
- As mentor and mentee undertake co-actions, such as co-planning and co-teaching, the mentee is able to engage in pedagogical practices that would not be accessible if they were working independently. The insights developed in this process then provide the foundation for increasing independent practice.
- Mentors and mentees work as a team, constantly passing ideas and roles back and forth in the creation of plans or in the implementation of learning. Co-acting is not the coming together of two independent actors, rather it is a unified process from beginning to end

3 Simple Steps

See page 55 for the Co-acting for Learning template.

1. Together, mentor and mentee go over and discuss the foundations, actions, and rewards of Co-acting for Learning on the template on page 55.
2. Together, mentor and mentee set the learning priorities for planning and teaching with ongoing discussion about instructional strategies, student

learning needs, resources, and assessment. With priorities in place, they collaboratively undertake the actual planning and teaching as co-action.

3. Mentor and mentee end with an assessment of the collaborative lesson or action they planned and implemented together, using evidence of student learning to support their conclusions.

Next Steps

- Remember the advantages of co-acting as you continue to work as a team.
- Refer to Mentoring Move: Inquiring Collaboratively (page 76) and Mentoring Move: Opening Up Practice (page 88) to find other strategies for supporting collaborative learning in professional settings.
- Expand your co-action network to include other mentors and mentees. Grade partners are also great collaborators. Such collaborations support professional development for teachers and successful learning outcomes for students.

How might I make visible to a mentee the thinking and rationale that underpin my teaching?

Making Your Thinking Visible

Teaching is an intricate process. It takes time and patience, trial and error, and resilience to build a strong foundation of knowledge and skills. Then, just when you think you have it figured out, new theories emerge that require teachers to continue our journey as learners and mentees, as well as teachers and mentors. A mentor who is able to make their thinking about theory and practice visible provides a mentee with support and encouragement to do likewise.

Stories from the Field: My Changing Voice (Diane)

When Wilhelm (2001) introduced "think aloud strategies" for use in the classroom, I jumped on the bandwagon. It seemed so logical to me to share my thinking with my students to help them learn to make meaning of text. During read-alouds, I would pause to share my thought processes about using the vivid language in a text to help me visualize the author's meaning, or to share strategies such as rereading portions of a text when the meaning was not immediately clear to me. I would stop to make connections to my experience, to other texts, or to the world around me. Students in my class seemed to be internalizing the play-by-play I was giving as we were reading, especially one young man who was constantly waving his hand at me to indicate he had a connection to the text that he wanted to share. However, I also noticed that the pure joy of a story was often lost in interruptions to the flow of the narrative.

Then another problem arose! At home, my children mentioned that I had started talking to myself as I was going about my household chores. I assured them that I was simply practicing thinking aloud, but it didn't seem to assuage their concern. I began to realize that my play-by-play in thinking aloud had presumed that every student needed to know how I was engaging with texts to read successfully. I was using a one-size-fits-all philosophy that was inappropriate and, for many students, unnecessary. I began to consider ways to probe and question students to make their thinking visible while also stimulating their curiosity about what others, including me, were thinking about the learning that was happening in our classroom. Our classroom moved to a place of *rich talk* (Vetter, 2008) that was significantly more inclusive and interesting for all of us.

For me, it was a short leap to bringing these classroom strategies to my role as a mentor. As I encouraged mentees to share their thinking with probes and questions, they soon became comfortable probing my thinking about pedagogy and classroom strategies that they did not understand. Rather than overwhelming mentees and students with information they didn't necessarily need, we were able to focus our limited conversation time in very practical ways for each mentee or student or situation. As a bonus, I don't talk to myself at home any more...at least, not as often.

The strategies presented here work well for both mentor and mentee to open the door to visible thinking. While mentees clearly need to understand the thinking that underpins the mentor's daily decision-making in the classroom, the mentor will also benefit from knowing the understandings (or misunderstandings) that account for successes and challenges as the mentee plans and implements classroom learning.

1. Encourage the use of questions that require deeper thinking in response. Use question starters such as "How would..." or "Why might..." to foster higher-level thinking. The Q-chart, a popular and commonly used classroom tool, based on Bloom's Taxonomy (Bloom, 1956) and adapted by Wiederhold (1998), helps students dig deeper into learning. It also promotes insights for mentors and mentees as they seek to analyze and synthesize the practice and theory that they engage with in the classroom.

Adapted from Wiederhold (1998)

Q-Chart

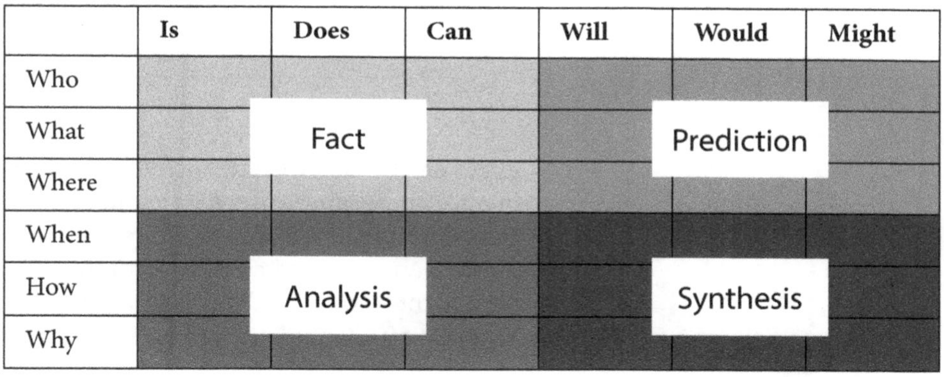

	Is	Does	Can	Will	Would	Might
Who						
What		Fact			Prediction	
Where						
When						
How		Analysis			Synthesis	
Why						

2. Demonstrate genuine interest, open-mindedness, and curiosity that invite questioning. Teachers are busy and may not have time to answer a mentee's question in the moment. To ensure the mentee knows you welcome their questions, invite them to discuss the question at a specific time later in the day or via online chats that can be responded to at a convenient time.
3. Welcome responses that are outside the box by exploring the implications. Often it seems easier to dismiss a new concept or idea than to find time to try something untested. Mentors and mentees should have a clear understanding that not all new ideas can be implemented due to time constraints; however, you can jointly prioritize a list of new ideas to implement those that seem most promising.

An important consideration in making thinking visible in a mentoring or classroom context is the availability of language. Education has a distinct discourse that has the potential to exclude a mentee from sharing your thinking. When planning a lesson, teacher euphemisms like "Student A works best independently," may not be clearly understood; a preservice or novice mentee may need to hear, "I observed that Student A doesn't seem to work well in a group. Let's brainstorm how we might support some collaborative learning skills." A mentee who is puzzling over the usage of buzz words or unfamiliar terminology will not have the confidence to fully engage in the conversation, and subsequently in the learning. Remember that acronyms that teachers use in one district may not be the same in another. Be sure to take time to understand a mentee's perspective. Perhaps a mentee has been educated or employed in a system that differs greatly from the one with which you are familiar. Ensure that a mentee has the opportunity to make their thinking visible to you so that learning can be a reciprocal process.

Stories from the Field: Windows into Difference (Diane)

A mentor called me with a concern that, despite having made visible his collaborative classroom practices and his rationale for using technology in the classroom, his mentee seemed to favor direct instruction and rarely made use of technology. A subsequent two-sided sharing of experience and practice revealed that the mentee had been educated in a school where technology resources were not available. All teaching had been direct and chalk-based. The unfamiliarity of a technology-rich collaborative learning environment was overwhelming to the mentee. As a result of the conversation, the mentor and mentee laid out a progressive plan to allow the mentee to gradually develop confidence in implementing collaborative learning and technology in the classroom.

In times of stress, it is common to fall back on acquired learning from past experience, rather than to implement newly learned and less familiar practice. If a mentee's past experience with learning does not reflect current district practices, then their mentor should tactfully approach the conversation to help the mentee develop an increased comfort with the unfamiliar. It is also a great opportunity for a mentor to learn about learning in other districts or parts of the world, and how that affects students who are newcomers to our classrooms.

Mentoring Move: Thinking Aloud

Thinking Aloud Is Key

- Think-aloud protocol design was originally introduced for use in product testing (Lewis, 1982) to allow researchers a window into user thinking. It was adapted to education (Wilhelm, 2001) as a means to support student learning and allow teachers to model their thought processes.
- This Mentoring Move asks mentors to engage their metacognitive processes and think aloud about their thinking; i.e., to express the rationale and often-subconscious analysis that underpins pedagogical decisions, such as the selection of instructional strategies and resources, or the design of lesson plans or physical environments. Mentors and mentees will benefit from explicit understanding of rationale that can be later assessed in the context of learning outcomes.

"(Mentors) do a lot of things that are very automated and we need those steps broken down for us, and made explicitly clear... Why you did that instead of this... Or why you changed the classroom around from last week to this week. Tell me what wasn't working, why you believe this is going to work. Just small things like that make a real difference for us."
— Teacher Candidate, 2017

3 Simple Steps

See page 56 for the Thinking Aloud template.

1. Mentors and mentees review the Insights from Research on the Thinking Aloud template on page 56. Consequently, they commit to thinking aloud to make explicit their thinking as they design, plan, implement, and assess learning for students. A mutual understanding of the purpose is important to ensure that neither feel that the commitment to think aloud is a means of oversight or judgment.
2. Mentor and mentee make "aside" comments to provide a window into thinking, when appropriate. Clearly the flow of a lesson or student interaction should not be interrupted by thinking aloud with the mentor or mentee. However, jot notes of questions or practices that need explanation can be saved until an opportunity presents itself later in the day.
3. Mentor and mentee discuss how thinking aloud leads to deeper thinking into practice and provides the opportunity for shared and individual reflection. Subsequent to such reflection, mentor and mentee may find that the simple articulation of thought results in an "aha!" moment that sparks new ideas and becomes a catalyst for further analysis.

Next Steps

- Mentors and mentees will both benefit from familiarizing themselves with the practice of thinking aloud, which is easily transferable to supporting student learning by demonstrating the metacognitive processes of learning.
- Think-aloud should be viewed as a strategy to help the mentee develop deeper understanding, rather than as a shortcut through the hard work of analyzing and synthesizing research and its relevance to practice.
- Presume only the best intentions of your mentoring partner as they think aloud. Honor the reality that you are being invited into a personal space. Avoid judgment by understanding that a misplaced word or a not-yet-fully-developed thought is common when thinking aloud.

How might I communicate effective feedback on classroom practice and processes?

Targeted Feedback

One of the first things that we make clear to new teachers is the importance of feedback. Many are initially terrified of the feedback process, seeing it as a judgment of them as a person, rather than an opportunity to gain insights into improving their practice. It is interesting to note that this is a common concern in fields that require extensive practical fieldwork (education, medicine, social work, etc.). Giving a learner a low grade on a written assignment may result in frustration, but it is generally recognized as an indicator that the work needs improvement, not as an indicator of the intelligence or the value of the person. In contrast, feedback perceived as negative in a mentoring situation often results in feelings of lower self-esteem or self-worth in terms of professionalism. While a poor grade on a paper may generate a determination to do better next time, negative feedback on practical performance often results in mentees questioning themselves and their ability to succeed in the profession.

An upfront conversation to establish a common understanding of feedback as a process undertaken to stimulate growth will help a mentee receive feedback in an open manner. Talk to your mentee about how getting feedback makes each of you feel; consider how you might work together to share feedback in a manner that is comfortable. An open proactive approach will help mentors and mentees to consider feedback as a means of growth, rather than a judgment. To ensure that feedback is seen in a positive light, we advocate for a process in which feedback is not simply given, but freely shared and requested by both mentor and mentee during the mentoring relationship.

We strongly support feedback that is objective, focused, and targeted to specific lessons or practices. To achieve that, it is important to avoid one-word evaluations, such as "great," "fine," or "okay." Rarely is a lesson 100% great, 100% fine, or 100% okay; therefore, a one-word response is, at best, incomplete or simply inaccurate. It is easy to give feedback when a lesson goes well. Among the positive comments, some areas for improvement might be mentioned, but if both mentor and mentee are happy with the outcome of the lesson, it is not difficult to address the few issues. The bigger challenge in providing feedback is when a lesson doesn't go well. To ease the stress of providing feedback in that situation, we need to consider how a mentor and mentee might collaborate to generate meaningful feedback.

Let's look at an example of a lesson that is being co-planned and co-taught by a mentor and mentee. The lesson was carefully planned and the implementation followed the plan in the classroom. However, students seemed to lack engagement in the learning, there were a lot of questions that indicated confusion on the part of students and, as the lesson drew to a close, it was clear that many students had not internalized the learning. Sound familiar? Sometimes lessons just don't go well! For teachers who are consistently growing and learning, there will be risk-taking in pedagogy that will result in the occasional lesson that flops. When this happens, it is not about poor teaching; it is a reality of being an ongoing learner who is willing to take risks to explore new pedagogy while working with diverse students and evolving curriculum.

Both the mentee and the mentor need to believe that, in spite of a bad lesson, they are not bad teachers. It is important to distinguish the difference. A bad lesson is an incident. The label of bad teacher runs the risk of becoming an identity. An incident is in the past and can be improved upon for the future. An identity inhabits the present and is more difficult to turn around. Objective, evidence-based feedback that is focused on what is observed during the lesson allows mentor and mentee to assess the work, rather than evaluate the person. Here are some questions to help with an objective analysis that will result in targeted feedback.

Planning

- What did we observe when introducing the lesson?
- How do we know if students demonstrated interest or found relevance in the lesson?
- How might we have changed the plan to better hook the students into the learning right from the start of the lesson?
- What observations demonstrated an understanding (or lack of understanding) of the learning objectives?
- How might the plan have been revised to ensure the flow of the lesson gave students the opportunity to understand the *what, how,* and *why* of the learning as the lesson unfolded?

Student Engagement

- What did we observe as the students engaged with the learning?

- Were there external issues at play (Friday afternoon, repeated interruptions, technology, etc.)?
- At what point did we observe confusion?
- What examples of student work or questions indicated they were successful or challenged by the learning?
- How might we have reworked the plan to mitigate the challenges we observed?

Assessment of Learning

- What can we learn from the observations, assessment of student work, and/or anecdotal notes that we took during the lesson?
- How might alternate assessment methods (oral, visual, groupings, etc.) have impact on the final result?

Often issues that arise in the mentoring process are not strictly lesson- or curriculum-based. For example, many new teachers struggle with challenges that extend across more than one lesson, and it is important for mentor and mentee to be able to ask for a conversation targeted on how to address the challenge. Mentoring Move: Targeted Feedback allows either mentor or mentee to highlight one particular issue and seek input to support growth.

Next Steps

- How might we move ahead to provide students with additional opportunities to consolidate their learning?

Working through these questions will allow mentors and mentees to formulate feedback on the lesson that is objective, logical, and evidence-based. It will result in recognition of both the positive and the negative aspects of the lesson. Evidence-based observations will also take the focus off the person and put it onto the lesson.

Mentoring Move: Targeted Feedback

Feedback Is Key

"I think then in hindsight . . . he didn't know and I'm expecting him to know."
— Mentor Teacher, 2017

- Feedback provides important insight to learners and to their mentors, who may presume that a mentee has knowledge, skills, or a comfort level with theory that, in reality, is not present. Often, we think of feedback flowing from a "more-knowledgeable other" (mentor) to a learner (mentee). In a true mentoring partnership, feedback can flow both ways. In fact, such reciprocal feedback strengthens the partnership. Targeted feedback opens the door to a collaborative exchange of thinking.
- Mentors and mentees have the opportunity to use targeted feedback when a specific concern is overshadowed by other successes or issues and has yet to be addressed. It can be initiated by either party.
- Targeted feedback involves either mentor or mentee identifying a concern, observing for specific feedback and recording the subsequent feedback, and determining next steps.

3 Simple Steps

See page 57 for the Targeted Feedback template.

1. Either mentor or mentee can initiate targeted feedback by identifying the concern or issue and writing it into the Targeted Feedback template on page 57 to explain the thinking that leads to the request.
2. A request for targeted feedback might lead to specific observation over a few days or rely on evidence from past lessons and teaching practice. Feedback looks at the practice, not the person, noting positive aspects as well as challenges or concerns, and is always supported by evidence. Targeted feedback is recorded on the template and discussed between mentor and mentee.

3. Analysis of the feedback and detailed supporting evidence completes the feedback process. Targeted feedback requires planning to discuss potential next steps for improvement and an action plan to facilitate improved practice.

Next Steps

- A busy classroom day often leaves little time for specific feedback. Good intentions may result in brief comments, such as "great day," rather than specific statements that lead to true improvement. Make time to share daily feedback that is meaningful, even if it is brief.
- Mentor and mentee need to take time to consider the feedback conversation and follow up together. Perspectives can change with time for contemplation. New ideas for addressing areas of concern or further enhancing strengths may later come to mind and should be shared.

How might I support mentees in self-assessing skills development?

Supporting Self-Assessment

We strongly believe that the best way to support new teachers in developing their skills is to support their ability to self-assess their practice from the first day of the mentoring relationship. Mentors who facilitate the independence of mentees in self-assessing their practice build preparedness for the professional responsibilities that lie ahead. Learning to self-assess practice and manage personal priorities in learning in the early days of teaching will lead to a significantly more satisfying and successful career.

The first step to fostering independence in self-assessing learning is to set clear parameters from the outset. Mentees could expect that a mentor will provide a virtual how-to manual for teaching, along with a checklist that indicates satisfactory or unsatisfactory performance. While this system might make life easier for a mentee in the initial stages, it creates greater problems down the road: the teacher continuing to self-assesses teaching against a simple checklist, waiting for someone else to evaluate their practice, or judging effective practice based solely on student results with a "the students passed so I must be doing a good job" mindset. A mentor with a view to the future helps a mentee to establish goals and work toward them. In the beginning, those goals might originate from a the university or college's description of learning outcomes, or a professional association guide for new teachers. Alternatively, categories might be abbreviated versions of the more detailed objectives of mentoring (see page 12).

For example, in distilling down objectives of mentoring to concise categories, a mentor and mentee might create a learning outcomes document with the following categories:

- Professionalism
- Communication and relationship-building
- Understanding learners, the learning environment, and the greater community
- Development of knowledge, skills, and strategies

Breakdowns of initial objectives within these categories might include the following:

Professionalism includes

- Familiarity with school protocols for attendance, emergencies, code of conduct, cell phone use, etc.
- Awareness of the professional requirements for teachers in the district

Communication and relationship-building include

- Awareness of Internet protocols, social media use, and electronic communications
- Interaction with other staff in the school and participation in school activities

Understanding learners, the learning environment, and the greater community includes

- Familiarity with the specific learning needs of students in the classroom
- Active engagement with the students in the learning environment
- Awareness of community priorities

Development of knowledge, skills, and strategies includes

- Familiarity with curriculum content
- Awareness of the impact of lesson planning on student success

Learning objectives must be part of a living document that initially establishes goals, then—as understandings, confidence, and practice grow—facilitates a progression of learning outcomes that reflect new objectives. For example, the goal of *Active engagement with the students in the classroom* may evolve into *Initiation of learning engagements with specific learning outcomes for a small group of students.* Then it might later become *Co-planning of learning engagements from initiation through culmination and assessment.* Mentor and mentee can set a timeline for achievement of the learning outcomes, but the timeline is not based on a set calendar of events. Learning outcomes must be allowed to evolve at a pace that respects the value of deep understanding by the mentee.

Too often mentors and mentees feel that achievement is a race against a calendar that predetermines a quantitative measure of teaching; for example, *Four weeks into the mentoring partnership the mentee will teach 75% of the day.* We challenge this type of thinking, advocating instead for a qualitative measure that uses effectiveness of planning, initiating, differentiating, sustaining, culminating, and assessing student learning engagements. Our rationale is that rote teaching is neither responsive to student needs nor effective. Therefore, a quantitative measure of time spent in front of the class (75% of the day in week four) is an ineffective measure unless it includes qualitative learning outcomes. For example, mentees who effectively co-plan and co-teach relevant, inclusive, and responsive lessons for 50% of the day, every day, are developing and demonstrating pedagogy that specifically targets the needs of the students in their classrooms. These strong teaching skills can easily be extended to 75% or 100% of the day as planning becomes more efficient and stamina is developed.

As research into professional learning communities has demonstrated, the value of working collaboratively provides greater opportunities for learning. A concurrent qualitative skills focus means that, as the mentee becomes more proficient, mentor and mentee can alternate in leading the planning and implementation of learning engagements.

Of course, each partnership can have a totally different set of learning outcomes. A preservice mentee will require different learning outcomes than a mentee who is working with an equally experienced mentor to collaboratively implement new practices. However, in all cases, successfully co-created learning outcomes ensure

- A shared direction of learning for the partnership
- Outcomes that are clearly articulated and understood
- Growth in practice
- Ongoing assessment of progress as achievement leads to new outcomes

An assessment tool should be easy to use and provide a concise visual representation of the learning. It should also allow for straightforward comparisons between prior and concurrent assessment to facilitate understanding of where growth has occurred and where the focus of learning needs should lie. An assessment tool should be primarily a self-assessment tool that can be used as a basis for conversation between mentor and mentee. Finally, an assessment tool needs to provide the opportunity to indicate progress along a continuum. Rather than a checklist-style assessment that may limit the opportunity for assessment to a Yes or No, we recommend a tool that provides a quick visual comparison and opportunities for conversations about challenges, areas for development, and successful elements.

Mentoring Move: Stoplight Self-Assessment

Self-Assessment Is Key

"Coming together provides a space to talk and reflect about our progress."
— Teacher Candidate, 2017

- Professional educators are responsible for designing, implementing, and assessing their practice. While a system of appraisal could be in place in certain jurisdictions, such appraisals might happen only once every few years. Therefore, it is imperative that professional educators assess their professional practice on an ongoing basis to ensure quality education.
- Stoplight Self-Assessment allows mentors and mentees to assess their practice in terms of set criteria using the color of common street signs as visual representation. See Stoplight Self-Assessment template on page 58.

3 Simple Steps

See page 58 for the Stoplight Self-Assessment template.

1. Mentors and mentees collaboratively create a specific set of success criteria that is relevant to their practice. For example, for a preservice mentee the elements might be drawn directly from the faculty's required learning outcomes; for a mentee who has been recently hired, a list of district priorities (e.g., guided reading, effectively using math manipulatives, etc.) might provide the basis for the success criteria.
2. Using the Stoplight Self-Assessment template on page 58, the mentee undertakes self-assessment of practice by highlighting the selected criteria with green, yellow, or red highlighter:

   - Green indicates the criteria are being met and the mentee should proceed.
   - Yellow indicates that some caution is required: *You are basically on track but you need to enhance your understanding.*
   - Red indicates that a full stop is required to look very carefully at the practice and determine next steps to further develop understandings.

   The highlighted document provides an immediate visual assessment of where some (balance of green, yellow, and red) or much (largely yellow and red) work is needed and where practice is flowing well (largely yellow and green). Steps are then planned to facilitate improvement where needed.
3. The process is undertaken again two to three weeks after the initial self-assessment. If progress is being made, you should see fewer red highlights,

perhaps a stable number of yellow as red becomes yellow and yellow becomes green, and a greater number of green highlights.

Next Steps

- It is important that responsibility for self-assessment remains with the person who is self-assessing, although input into criteria used for self-assessment might be contributed by a mentoring partner.
- Once self-assessment indicates that focus criteria have been met, a new round of self-assessment can begin with new success criteria. For example, an initial self-assessment might begin with a focus on success criteria related to lesson planning. Subsequent self-assessment could reflect criteria that focus on student engagement, use of technology, or another specific area of focus determined to be relevant to practice.

How might I help mentees identify their specific needs?

Identifying Needs

The following typical mentor/mentee conversation might seem familiar to you. We have heard it echoed by countless mentees and related by many mentors as they work through the process of mentoring.

> Mentor: I am really looking forward to working with you. What can I do that will be most helpful?
> Mentee: Just tell me what I need to know.
> Mentor: What specifically do you think you need to know?
> Mentee: I have no idea... I don't even know what I don't know!

In our experience, a significant challenge for mentors and mentees lies in analyzing our learning needs. We would argue that the greatest possibility for development and growth results from a place of not knowing. This is the place where the mentor and the art of mentorship flourish, as mentors support mentees in self-assessing their areas of greatest need.

In this context it is helpful to identify these opportunities for learning:

- What you know: This is current knowledge you possess and can expand upon. For example, you might have knowledge about lesson planning, but can expand upon your learning by seeking out resources and research for new types of lesson design; for example, backward design (Wiggins & McTighe, 1998).
- What you know you don't know: This is a gap in your learning that you recognize and can fill by taking steps to pursue and develop your understandings. For example, you have heard of differentiated instruction and recognize you know nothing about it. Your awareness of this gap in your understanding allows you to take action to learn.

Practice in the art of metacognitive thinking allows us to look at what we think we know and what we know we don't know to come up with a reasonable learning plan to satisfy our needs. If you are not familiar with the process of metacognitive thinking (or thinking about your thinking), check out Chapter 4 and Mentoring Move: Opening Up Practice on page 88.

Mentees often come to the classroom with a clear understanding of what they think they know. Some of that understanding might have come from experience as a student; therefore, the perspective might differ from that of the mentor. It is important to recognize that having a different perspective does not make either party wrong. It is simply a matter of listening to the other to clarify what they think they know, and how and why they think they know it, and being open to amending what they think they know in order to gain a more fully developed understanding and alternate perspectives. The point is that knowledge gaps are generally concrete and fillable.

A greater concern arises when we are dealing with competencies. We would argue that gaps in competencies have much greater impact on a new teacher's ability to meet the demands of the profession than gaps in knowledge. While some people are able to identify some gaps in their competencies (e.g., I am not good at challenging conversations; I don't do well doing something solo and work best as part of a team), it is generally the competency gaps that are most difficult to self-assess.

We have identified key core competencies as being

- Critical Analysis: The ability to consider issues from multiple perspectives and delve deeply into one's understandings to reveal personal experiences and biases that may influence the conclusions drawn.
- Teamwork: The ability to work within a team environment as an effective collaborator, contributor, and critical thinker.
- Communication: The ability to effectively communicate in writing, orally, and electronically.
- Problem-solving: The ability to define issues and to analyze and implement solutions.

Clearly, it is not the role of the mentor to analyze a mentee and point out their personal shortcomings. However, a skilled mentor will be able to use probing questions to help a mentee look inside themselves and determine where they need to focus their attention in developing their core competencies.

It is important to recognize that a gap in one's competencies does not make someone incompetent. Rather, it is a strength to recognize and self-assess competency gaps and to work to close those gaps. Facilitated conversation with a mentor who is able to ask probing questions will support mentees as they explore ways of further developing their competencies. Self-discovery by mentees is significantly more productive and easier to process than a needs analysis by a mentor.

Mentoring Move: Needs Analysis

Self-Awareness Is Key

"I don't like to have a checklist, as that's not what (my teacher candidate) needs."
— Mentor Teacher, 2017

- Needs analysis allows mentors and mentees to focus on what they need to best facilitate learning for students and to optimally contribute to the professional mentoring relationship.
- Beyond lesson-planning skills and assessment knowledge that facilitate the implementation of learning in the classroom, cognitive requirements include the ability to problem-solve, to make sound judgments, to assess situations, and to make decisions that are necessary for professional accomplishment and favorable learning outcomes.
- Using the Needs Analysis template on page 59 to consider knowledge and skill-based needs, as well as cognitive requirements, mentors and mentees develop a mutual understanding of their needs and the needs of the other within the

professional context. The objective is to help mentees determine within the core competencies what is most pressing, what they are wondering about, and, finally, what would be nice to chat about. This prioritizing of needs leads to the development of a concrete plan of action.

3 Simple Steps

See page 59 for the Needs Analysis template.

1. Mentors and mentees access current information about specific categories of knowledge, core competencies, and skills to identify and assess their specific areas of need; use the Needs Analysis template on page 59.
2. Mentors and mentees collaboratively brainstorm to consider how to best access appropriate strategies to support their development in the required areas.
3. Mentors and mentees create an action plan to support the needs of both. Action plan items might include an ongoing sharing of feedback (see Mentoring Move: Targeted Feedback on page 47), accessing resources or research to provide additional insights, liaising with faculty of education partners for mentoring support or professional development, or undertaking a lesson study or professional inquiry (see Mentoring Move: Inquiring Collaboratively on page 76). The action plan would also determine a date for review on progress.

Next Steps

- Take advantage of professional development opportunities within the work environment in addition to independent research to further develop mastery of the knowledge, skills, or cognitive requirements required by the profession.
- Take the initiative to work within the greater mentoring community to share understandings, create reciprocal learning opportunities, and/or launch inquiry groups to address specific needs that may be common to the community.

Articulation to Action

"Aha!" Moments	Clarifications	Shared Philosophies

Opportunities to enhance practice and student learning:

Co-acting for Learning

Foundations of a co-acting partnership in the classroom include

- Mutual respect
- Flexibility
- Open-mindedness
- Willingness
- Working toward a common learning objective for students
- Listening to new ways of doing and being in the classroom
- Taking responsible risks with new pedagogy
- Thinking critically about your personal perspective and lens
- Recognizing your biases toward specific ways of learning/being in the classroom
- Open communication

Co-acting includes

- Co-planning
- Co-teaching
- Collaboration to set learning objectives to meet student needs
- Collaborative inquiry
- Sharing ideas
- Sharing resources
- Moderated marking/assessment
- Communication relevant to
    - Instructional strategies
    - Prior knowledge
    - Experience
    - Personal interests/strengths
    - Professional learning objectives
- Generating what-if scenarios to take risks in pedagogy that have the potential to expand professional learning and student learning

Rewards of participating in a co-acting partnership in the classroom include

- Professional growth and development for both mentor and mentee
- Infusion of energy, new ideas, and pedagogies in the classroom
- Enhanced engagement in and satisfaction with the work of the classroom when the successes and challenges of both mentor and mentee are shared

Thinking Aloud

Insights into Research

Constructing understanding requires both cognitive and metacognitive elements. Learners "construct knowledge" using cognitive strategies, and they guide, regulate and evaluate their learning using metacognitive strategies. It is through this "thinking about thinking", this use of metacognitive strategies, that real learning occurs. As students become more skilled at using metacognitive strategies, they gain confidence and become more independent as learners.

— Literacy Information and Communication System; retrieved from https://lincs.ed.gov/state-resources/federal-initiatives/teal/guide/metacognitive

The ability to self-regulate learning is essential for teachers' professional growth during their entire career as well as for their ability to promote these processes among students.
Kramarski & Michalsky, 2009, p. 161

Thinking aloud provides mentors the opportunity to engage their metacognitive processes and make them apparent to mentees.

Pembroke Publishers ©2020 *Mentoring Each Other* by Lana Parker and Diane Vetter ISBN 978-1-55138-346-0

Targeted Feedback

1. Identify a specific question of practice or area of professional growth about which you would like to have targeted feedback.

2. Explain why this feedback is important to you.

3. Explain possible factors that you feel might be contributing to your uncertainty about your practice or growth in this area.
   -
   -
   -
   -

4. Agree on a date or period of time during which targeted feedback will occur.

5. Determine the types of evidence that will be useful in providing feedback about your question, issue, or area of growth. Mentor will collect evidence during the observation. Mentee will seek to be keenly aware of evidence of student engagement during the lesson to facilitate subsequent conversation.

6. Collaborate to analyze the evidence collected. To what extent does the evidence provide answers? What additional feedback might be required?

7. Create an action plan to determine next steps, implement new strategies, seek new resources and/or support improved practice.

Stoplight Self-Assessment

You will need:

- green, yellow and red highlighters
- a printed copy of the success criteria you will be self-assessing

Red means Stop: you need to develop a greater understanding.

Yellow means Caution: you are basically on track but you need to enhance your understanding.

Green means Go: you are on track and have met the specific criterion of the learning outcome.

A word of caution: If you have all or most criteria highlighted green, take a second look to ensure you have accurately assessed your practice. If so, you should up your game with new success criteria. Learning is never complete. It is a lifelong process.

Needs Analysis

Communication: Communicative competence includes the ability to share information effectively, using a range of technologies and media. It includes communication in writing and verbally, listening and asking questions to understand, and appreciating other points of view.

Teamwork: Being a good collaborator involves contributing to the team by sharing information and expertise. An effective collaborator provides feedback in a constructive manner, respecting diversity in people and perspectives.

Problem-Solving: Problem-solving requires defining and analyzing a problem to seek and assess potential solutions. When assessing a new situation and identifying problems, there is a need to communicate clearly with others, engage others in the decision-making process, and critically evaluate solutions.

Critical Analysis: Critical thinkers have the ability to explore an issue, problem, event, or idea in some depth before accepting or formulating an opinion, based on information that is credible and relevant. It requires examining your own and others' assumptions, formulating other points of view. and arriving at a thoughtful conclusion.

Adapted from ee_guide.info.yorku.ca *Experiential Education Guide - Core Competencies*

Core Competencies	**Needs**
Communication	Most pressing: Wondering about: Nice to chat about:
Teamwork	Most pressing: Wondering about: Nice to chat about:
Problem-Solving	Most pressing: Wondering about: Nice to chat about:
Knowledge/Skills	Most pressing: Wondering about: Nice to chat about:
Feedback	Most pressing: Wondering about: Nice to chat about:
Critical Thinking	Most pressing: Wondering about: Nice to chat about:
Resources	Most pressing: Wondering about: Nice to chat about:
Support/Connections	Most pressing: Wondering about: Nice to chat about:

Pembroke Publishers ©2020 *Mentoring Each Other* by Lana Parker and Diane Vetter ISBN 978-1-55138-346-0 

3

Reciprocal Learning

While reassuring new students that they will soon be immersed in the learning, we express our hope that they will never "master" the act, art, or science of teaching—for that would mean they have acquired complete knowledge and there is nothing left to learn. Our hope for all teachers is that they will continue to grow and learn throughout their teaching career. Learners benefit from teachers who are constantly curious, who are not convinced they know all there is to know. Classrooms need teachers who are always in pursuit of new learning, new ideas, and new ways to lead the evolution of education to meet the demands of a changing world.

So we turn our attention to maintaining a mentoring relationship by emphasizing reciprocal learning. Building on our earlier discussions of establishing a mentoring relationship and strategies, this chapter outlines the value of paying close attention to the power dynamic that characterizes a mentoring relationship. Our research into mentors and among teacher candidates has illustrated that, once the hierarchy of power between mentor and mentee has been addressed, the flow of communication improves, becoming more honest, authentic, and purposeful. As such, here we set the stage for a symbiotic relationship that allows for knowledge and questions to flow freely between mentor and mentee.

Historically, mentoring and teaching relationships have been characterized by a power imbalance. The mentor or teacher has been the knowledge holder, and the mentee or student has been the passive recipient. We find the assumptions about teaching and learning made by this traditional set of roles problematic. The first assumption is that mentors are all-knowing. The traditional power structure places the weight of knowing, of certainty, and of being an exemplary model squarely on the mentor's shoulders. As we noted in Chapter 1, this pressure to be perfect can lead to teaching being a performance—the Tuesday teacher—rather than authentic practice. The second assumption is that the learner, or mentee, has little of value to contribute to the knowledge exchange. It also permits the mentee to be a passive recipient in the exchange: *you give and I take.*

Of course, we know that real mentorship is messier than that. There can be unexpected surprises that lead to improvisation. Obstacles in the face of even the most well-planned lessons can lead to frustration. Different life experiences produce differing perspectives on what is most important in the classroom. But all of these experiences can become moments of insight and learning for both mentor and mentees, if approached with the right mindset.

To establish a reciprocal-learning mindset, we advocate that all mentoring relationships make time to **address the power structure** in the relationship, making efforts to transition away from traditional roles to a more open and balanced approach. A reciprocal learning mindset is also based upon responsiveness and mutual growth: **responsiveness** is the ability of both mentor and mentee to respond to each other's unique needs and goals; **mutual growth** is assured through the relationship when both learners have the opportunity to satisfy their needs and make progress toward their professional goals. Once the stage has been set for a reciprocal flow of knowledge, we can open ourselves and our practice to more **risk-taking**. Of course, an open and balanced approach means that we may have to spend some time **negotiating differences**: How can different values find common ground? How can a mentee contribute to an existing classroom environment? How can a mentor adjust plans to incorporate new ideas? Finally, a reciprocal learning mindset can produce opportunities for profound growth and new **professional learning** through collaborative research.

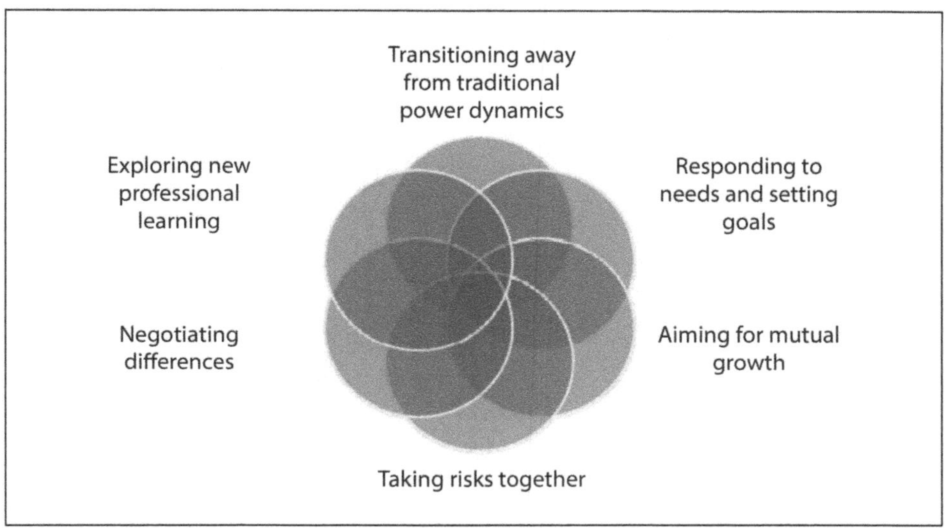

To foster a relationship of reciprocal learning, we consider these key questions:

- How might we transition from the traditional expert/novice roles to partners in learning? Why is this shift important? (See page 62.)
- How might the mentoring partnership respond to the unique needs and qualities of the mentor and mentee? (See page 64.)
- How do we make the mentoring experience mutually rewarding and beneficial for the mentor and mentee? (See page 66.)
- How might mentoring support me in taking productive risks to facilitate growth for students, my mentee, and myself? (See page 69.)
- How do we negotiate difference? (See page 71.)
- How might action research and inquiry facilitate mentor and mentee professional learning? (See page 75.)

How might we transition from the traditional expert/novice roles to partners in learning? Why is this shift important?

Transitioning from Traditional Power Dynamics

Mentoring relationships are traditionally thought of as hierarchies, with the mentor, as expert, holding more power than a mentee, as novice. According to this model, a mentor might possess expertise, set the rules, and evaluate the outcomes. In education, while there are myriad mentoring relationships, most conform to some variation of the power balance described above. Experienced teachers mentor teacher candidates, but they are also quite likely responsible for evaluating them. Induction mentors are often tasked with assuring that new teachers will be successful in a school. Administrators who mentor their junior colleagues might have a voice in their performance evaluation or in a future promotion process. It's no wonder that a power balance exists! Nevertheless, with mutual goodwill, each individual mentoring relationship can deconstruct the hierarchy at the core of the traditional relationship and move into a more balanced and equitable partnership. The goal is to evolve away from a relationship characterized by obedience and passive receptiveness, and toward an exchange of ideas that benefits both partners. A mentor might be more experienced and knowledgeable about classroom practice. But a mentee can bring their previous experience, education, and new perspectives to the relationship. The goal of reciprocal learning is to recognize the value in both.

Stories from the Field: A Mentee's Practicum Experience (Lana)

When Natalie was a teacher candidate, her first two practicum experiences were an exercise in frustration. The first practicum was in a Grade 3 class. The Mentor Teacher was very knowledgeable and organized, and when they first met Natalie thought that she was going to learn a lot from her mentor. But on the second day of the month-long block, the teacher asked if Natalie felt comfortable teaching for the full day for the remainder of the month. There was a perceptible power imbalance, and Natalie felt compelled to say yes. For the remainder of that month, she drew on her existing experience and knowledge to develop a full program for the students. And while she learned, it was only from her students, who provided her with very honest feedback each day through their level of engagement. Her mentor might have trusted her, but the power imbalance in their relationship and the mentor's insistence that Natalie work independently meant that her learning was limited to trial and error in the classroom.

Natalie's second practicum experience was a variation on the same theme. But in lieu of being left to her own devices, this mentor handed her a binder for the month and asked that Natalie follow it each day. Once again, Natalie's greatest learning came from her interactions with students. She may have gained some new resources (from the binder), but wasn't able to plan anything or make adaptations. She was stuck performing in someone else's teaching skin.

In her last practicum, Natalie finally had the experience she was hoping for. The Mentor Teacher asked her what she was interested in teaching, based on her existing strengths and curiosity. He took the lead for half the day, sharing his resources and his thinking with Natalie as the day progressed. He gave her autonomy to lead for the other half of the day, making time to debrief at the end of the day so that she could make adjustments. While they didn't always see eye to eye, Natalie learned more from him than from either of her previous mentors because they talked about all aspects of classroom practice.

The first two experiences described are, sadly, all too common. As practicum supervisors, we have had many discussions about how to navigate practicum with a Mentor Teacher who is either too laid-back or too controlling. The fatal flaw in the first two situations is that neither Mentor Teacher modelled any kind of open communication. Their expertise was wasted because it couldn't be accessed in any meaningful or transparent way. And unfortunately, with a traditional power imbalance, mentees can be trapped in silence, performing with limited support.

Meaningful mentoring must begin by addressing the power dynamic. The greatest obstacle to learning is the suppression of one party through fear—of being judged, of failing. For mentors, as the traditional power-holders, a good starting point is to acknowledge your mentee's existing knowledge. A warm welcome into a discussion will help a mentee feel right from the start that their knowledge is of value and worth sharing. A mentor can also explicitly invite the mentee to provide feedback about the mentoring process. If a mentee knows they can approach their mentor with a request, then some of the fear of being judged might dissipate. Mentors and mentees could also find it helpful to spend time at the very start of the relationship outlining how feedback and evaluation might be structured, especially if a formal evaluation is involved.

Mentoring Move: What I Bring

Giving Is Key

"I wanted to learn things. I wanted to be responsible and to be the best I can be for that person."
— Mentor Teacher, 2017

- The objective of this Mentoring Move is to facilitate an understanding that both mentor and mentee have something valuable to give to the mentoring relationship, regardless of their years of experience or lack thereof. Mentor and mentee discover that both have much to share and that learning can be reciprocal.
- What I Bring asks mentors and mentees to reflect on what they have to give to the mentoring relationship, including traits, characteristics, interests, hobbies, specific knowledges, ways of knowing, and habits of mind that have the potential to have a positive effect on the mentoring relationship.

3 Simple Steps

See page 78 for the What I Bring template.

1. Mentors and mentees reflect on what they bring to the mentoring relationship and what they can give to the partnership. It is important to consider both personal and professional attributes.
2. Draw the outline of a tree on chart paper or use the graphic on the What I Bring template on page 78. Mentor and mentee write one attribute per sticky note. (Sticky notes colored like fall leaves provide the best visual effect.) Attributes are then affixed to the tree to give the appearance of a display of a tree in fall color.
3. Together, mentor and mentee reflect on the attributes. Questions for reflection might include:
    - What unique attributes are on our tree?
    - How might we use these attributes to enhance our work in the classroom and contribute to student learning?
    - In what ways might we learn from each other?

Next Steps

- Continue to value the experiences and expertise that both mentee and mentor possess to support reciprocal learning.

- Seek ways to infuse what mentor and mentee bring in term of talents, skills, and new knowledge into collaborative lesson planning and classroom inquiries.
- Use this Mentoring Move with students in the classroom. Ask students to reflect on what they bring to the classroom and to their relationship with their teachers and peers to remind them of their responsibility to the classroom environment and to support relationship-building. Valuing what students can bring to the teaching and learning experience fosters in them a sense of ownership of and engagement with classroom interactions and learning.

How might the mentoring partnership respond to the unique needs and qualities of the mentor and mentee?

Responding to Each Other's Needs

Teachers make hundreds of decisions in a day; the profession requires consistent and ongoing decision-making. Let's break that down a bit. Each day, teachers coordinate a plan, offer instruction, and enact evaluations with some intention. Larger decisions might comprise the content of the plan, the choice of resources, and the range of instructional and assessment methods. Smaller decisions, which are no less influential, include how to respond in a moment of uncertainty (like when a lesson is falling flat or a student asks an unexpected question) and how to navigate day-to-day interactions among students and with colleagues.

But how do all these decisions get made? Teaching comes from a deeply personal place. It emerges from an intersection of knowledge and experiences, beliefs and values, and personal qualities. Often, experienced teachers are so practiced, they don't even realize they are making decisions anymore. But that fluency comes at a cost: a lack of awareness of why they are choosing certain actions over others and a kind of blinkered vision that might prevent them from seeing available alternatives. Somewhere in proficiency lies the danger of an unthinking automaticity.

For a mentoring partnership to succeed, then, the goal is to probe some of that automaticity—that fluency of practice—to ask why. Why did you choose that? Why did you undertake that action? Why, in that moment, was that the right choice? With probing, we can uncover our underlying philosophy, our beliefs, and our values. A strong reciprocal partnership begins with some insight (and maybe some common ground) in these areas.

Stories from the Field: Ships in the Night (Lana)

Linda came to my office in tears. She was a teacher candidate who had already had a lengthy career outside of education and was returning to university to get a teaching degree. She had just begun a practicum placement in a new classroom. Her mentor teacher was very experienced and had been hosting teacher candidates for a number of years. Linda told me the source of her frustration: she was trying to incorporate some of the new teaching strategies she was learning about at the Faculty of Education into her daily practices. This included a range of grouping routines designed to get students out of their seats and talking. At the end of a couple of days of experimentation with the routines, Linda's mentor teacher shared critical feedback indicating that Linda seemed to be having issues with classroom structure, routine, and management.

Consider: What do you think Linda values? Does her mentor share those values? Does the mentor recognize the connection between Linda's instructional choices and her values?

Mentoring Move: Sharing Values helps establish some common ground on the basis of the mentoring relationship.

The analogy of ships in the night is pretty appropriate for Linda and her mentor. One thing evident from listening to Linda is that neither she nor her mentor had taken the time to discuss Linda's plan. More pressingly, neither had spent any time learning about the other's beliefs and values in the classroom. They were in the metaphorical dark in their conversations, moving further and further away from each other as misunderstanding grew into mistrust. For reciprocal learning to become a norm in a mentoring relationship, both parties must have intentional conversations about their values. The first step is to ask questions about what is valued within the mentoring relationship: what does the mentor value in a mentee and what does the mentee value in a mentor?

A second step is to establish what the other values broadly in education and, particularly, in the classroom. A reciprocal learning partnership must make the time and effort to learn about the beliefs that mobilize each partner's decisions. The following questions offer signposts to guide the conversation:

- Why is education important?
- What is the purpose of education?
- What three words would you choose to describe your goals as a teacher?
- What three words would you use to describe the ideal classroom?
- What do you hope students will learn over the course of a year in your classroom?
- How do you hope to engage students who might be struggling?
- What about your own experiences as a student informs your current teaching practice?

For further work in this area, have a look at Mentoring Move: Opening Up Practice on page 88.

Once these larger, more philosophical questions have been answered, the partnership can move on to uncovering the particular "whys" behind certain classroom practices and decisions.

Mentoring Move: Sharing Values

Sharing Is Key

"I liked just the sense of having a more planned approach to being a mentor teacher, because really in the past how I've approached it has just been, like, as how things come up in the craziness of the day. And I just felt, like, now I could do it a lot more justice."
— Mentor Teacher, 2017

- This Mentoring Move adapts thinking maps (Hyerle, 2008) to provide mentors and mentees with the opportunity to share the qualities they value most in their role and in the role of the other.
- Using the circle maps on Sharing Values, parts 1 and 2 on pages 79 and 80, mentors and mentees identify the personal traits, professional qualities, and personality characteristics they value in a mentor and in a mentee. While mentors and mentees may determine that they have differing values, the exercise of coming to know what the other values is of importance.

3 Simple Steps

See pages 79 and 80 for the Sharing Values templates.

1. Mentors and mentees use the Sharing Values, page 1 template on page 79 to create a circle map titled Mentor. On the Mentor map, mentors articulate what they value in a mentor in the middle circle as they view the role as *insiders*. Mentees do likewise in the outer circle as they view the Mentor role as *outsiders*.
2. Mentors and mentees repeat the process with the Sharing Values, page 2 template on page 80, creating a circle map titled Mentee. This time mentees write in the middle circle as they are the insiders who are central to the role, while mentors write on the outer circle.
3. Mentors and mentees study the two maps to see where values converge and differ. They then discuss what those values look like in the practical

environment. Mentor and mentee strive to understand the values that one or both perceive to be important to the role, and provide examples of why they are important. They ask:

- How might we use these attributes to enhance our work in the classroom and contribute to student learning?
- In what ways might we learn from each other?

Next Steps

- Ensure you fully understand what your mentor or mentee values so that you can honor that value in your work together. While the values that your partner identifies might not rank as highly on your list, respect each other's perspective. Demonstrate that respect in interactions.
- As mentors and mentees continue their work together, they reinforce the values as examples arise. For example, a mentor might have written *reliability* as something they value, noting that reliability looks like *Saying what you will do and doing what you say you will.* This is important to the mentor because students need to trust their teachers, and reliability is a core element of trust. Therefore, if you make a promise to students or tell them that you will do something, you need to follow through.

How do we make the mentoring experience mutually rewarding and beneficial for the mentor and mentee?

Aiming for Mutual Growth

We have noted that reciprocal learning requires us to address the power dynamic and to spend some time learning about one another's values. We have also acknowledged that a reciprocal learning mindset can produce positive outcomes for both parties involved in mentoring. Some of these benefits might be intangible, or *felt* outcomes. For example, one might experience decreased stress as a result of feeling less vulnerable and less subject to judgment. Or one might feel excitement at the prospect of finding some common ground in a values-building exercise. But for these benefits to become more tangible as an intentional manifestation of our engagement, we need to think deeply about our individual learning journeys and goals.

At the start of a mentoring journey, it is assumed that the mentee will be in a receptive state of mind, learning and acquiring new skills and knowledge through observation and engagement. And yet, there are still challenges. Despite being in a learning stance, the mentee might not be able to articulate what they want to learn more about. In the previous chapter, we described the usefulness of the Mentoring Move: Needs Analysis (page 52) to help guide structured conversations and feedback. Now, when considering reciprocal learning, we follow up that suggestion with an extension. Once some of the mentee's learning needs have been addressed and there is a decreased sense of urgency, it becomes useful to revisit the conversation about what the mentee hopes to learn more about.

A mentor, on the other hand, might not naturally assume a learning mindset. If traditional roles prevail, a mentor might perceive learning as a reflection of weakness or of absence of expertise. However, if the partnership is pursuing a reciprocal learning mindset, one of the most useful things a mentor can do—especially in conjunction with the conversation about values described on page 65—is to identify their own areas of interest and their own learning goals.

Parallel Learning

We use the term parallel learning here to help distinguish it from a more formal collaborative inquiry, which we discuss on page 75.

After using the Mentoring Move: Needs Analysis on page 52 or the Mentoring Move: Sharing Values on page 65, plan for a follow-up conversation to share recent experiences with professional learning, identify an area of ongoing interest, and commit to parallel learning. Parallel learning suggests that each party in the mentor pair can name and pursue their own area of interest, gaining expertise through both research and in-class experimentation, and then report back to one another. Parallel learning offers us a way to maintain our individual learning objectives while still having the support of a partner. It also furnishes us with a natural sense of responsibility and commitment to the learning.

In parallel learning, mentor and mentee each

- Identify some area of field of education that is of particular interest to them (once again, based on values and experiences)
- Trace their learning journey in that area
- Plan for future learning pathways
- Commit to a first check-in to share a bit about what they learned and to choose a strategy or tool they learned about to try in the classroom
- Commit to second check-in to report back on/debrief the classroom experience

Conversational prompts can help engage at each stage of the parallel learning pathway.

Identify

- What is an area of education research that interests me?
- Why might that area stand out as being of special interest?
- How might that area inform my current classroom practice?
- What do I value about that area of education research?

Some ideas for an area of focus could include differentiated instruction, assessment, working with students with exceptionalities, culturally responsive pedagogy, education technology, study of specific curriculum fields (e.g., mathematics, language, the arts, etc.), culturally and linguistically diverse communities, family–school partnerships, education psychology, modern learning (21st century and beyond), second-language learning and plurilingual contexts, creating classroom communities, race and education, backward design and planning.

Trace

- What do I already know about this area? How do I know it?
- How does it tie in to my own education and teaching background?
- What am I hoping to achieve by researching that area?

Plan

- What books, websites, courses, or professional development sessions might I choose to further my learning?
- What is the timeline?

First Check-In

- What have I learned so far?
- How does it fit with or add a new dimension to what I already knew?
- What has been surprising, troubling, and/or exciting about this new learning?
- What does my new learning mean for my current practice?
- What new strategies, tools, routines, processes, or infrastructure might I want to introduce?
- What am I hoping to see in my classroom?
- How will I gauge success?

Second Check-In

- What did I do?
- What went well? What didn't?
- What would I like to tweak for the next time?
- Would it be useful to continue to explore resources? If so, which ones?
- Is another check-in going to be helpful? If so, when should it be scheduled for?

Parallel learning fits perfectly with the goal of deconstructing power in a mentoring relationship and contributes nicely to putting each member of the pair into a learning mindset. It preserves and respects individual interests and trajectories by enabling each partner to choose an area and pathway that corresponds to their goals. It permits both teachers to personalize and differentiate based on their classrooms, which means that outcomes are likely to be relevant to students. Finally, parallel learning offers a structure for mutual growth and success by providing goals and a sense of accomplishment to both mentor and mentee.

Mentoring Move: I'd Like to Learn More About...

Parallel Learning Is Key

"Mentoring is and should be about intentional, purposeful practices that *both* mentor and mentee benefit from."
— Mentor Teacher, 2017

- This Mentoring Move provides us with a structure to identify individual learning goals that can be explored with the support of the mentor partnership. While a mentor and mentee might have different interests, take different courses, read different materials, and try different strategies in the classroom, a parallel learning structure provides the opportunity to report back, debrief, and brainstorm new paths forward.
- A parallel learning approach allows us to create and maintain some of our own space for learning and some autonomy. It also permits us to develop expertise in a specialized area, which is helpful in neutralizing the power imbalance.

3 Simple Steps

See page 81 for the I'd Like to Learn More About... template.

1. Use the chart on the I'd Like to Learn More About... template on page 81 to guide and chart your joint commitments. Each partner should follow the process of identifying an area of interest, pursuing research, and experimenting with new approaches in the classroom.
2. Be sure to make time for a debrief after the first classroom experiment. Talk about key themes as well as what actions you undertook in the classroom. Note any revisions or new ideas you have for the second phase.
3. Engage in a bit more research, refine your strategies, and take some different positive risks in the classroom.

Next Steps

- The objective of parallel learning is to involve each member of the partnership in an engaging exploration of a topic of interest. And while that learning originally begins with autonomous inquiries and research, it is quite likely that new strategies and tools will be shared. As a consequence, simply discussing and debriefing the research with one another is not necessarily a productive next step. Try out some of your partner's recommendations with your students.
- If a parallel learning structure has been successful, or if mentor's and mentee's areas of interest dovetail, a logical next step is to explore the Mentoring Move: Inquiring Collaboratively (see page 76) for a learning project with a shared focus.
- If you feel your learning might be valuable to your colleagues, share your ideas with administration and in team and staff meetings.

How might mentoring support me in taking productive risks to facilitate growth for students, my mentee, and myself?

Taking Risks Together

The mentoring partnership can become a wonderful space of experimentation, risk, and reward. If the relationship is grounded in a reciprocal learning mindset, then mentor and mentee become co-conspirators in a series of experiments. Take the example from Natalie's third practicum experience (see page 62): an ideal extension of that partnership would have been, not just to debrief the day's learning, but also to co-plan, with both the mentor and mentee taking chances with their practice.

For mentors, having a professional partner can refresh a practice. Even for a mentor who is working with new ideas and incorporating new strategies on a regular basis, having an outside perspective can shake up routine or rote practices. The key, of course, is remaining open to the potential for change. A mentor who is truly working toward reciprocal learning recognizes that they have the potential to learn and grow as much as their mentee. Both mentor and mentee are encouraged to perceive the mentoring process as a journey or adventure that can uncover surprising new ways of being in the classroom.

For mentees, risk has always been an inherent part of a mentoring process. As previously noted, when enacting traditional power structures in a mentoring relationship, the mentee might believe that they are undertaking most of the risk in the relationship. They might feel as though they are most vulnerable, exposing their novice practices to scrutiny, and risking real failure in the event they are being evaluated. For their part, mentors in a traditional hierarchal relationship may feel as if they are assuming the most risk by opening their classroom (in the case of Associate Teachers) or their best practices to someone else's gaze. Either way, the traditional model produces negative feelings or fear. It leads us to become more rigid, prescriptive, and tenuous.

A healthy mentoring relationship that is committed to reciprocal learning is characterized by an openness to trial and error, to trying out new approaches, and to honest discussion about outcomes. The risk, when shared between partners, takes on a new quality. It becomes a source of excitement and discovery; it suggests that curiosity leads to innovation, and that trying something new can produce great rewards.

Stories from the Field: Picture-Book Togetherness (Diane and Lana)

In one of our research groups, we invited mentor teachers and teacher candidates together to engage in professional development. On the second day, we asked both mentors and mentees to bring a picture book that they thought would be suitable for their class in preparation for a co-planning exercise. The results were very interesting.

When they had a resource to discuss—that is, a third point in the conversation—mentors and mentees were able not only to express their values and ideas, but also to share observations about students. We observed that, in some cases, a mentee brought a resource; in other cases, the mentor also brought a book. They read each other's suggestions and debated the suitability of one text over the other. In one pair, the two texts were found to have complementary themes, which led to excited discussions about co-planning. These books led to conversations about how to plan upcoming units, as well as discussions about how to accommodate and modify for particular students. We witnessed mentees researching course notes they felt could contribute to the unit. We also overheard mentors sharing ideas about how to bring parents and families into the learning.

But our most significant observation, as researchers, was the shift in energy in the room. Our mentor-and-mentee teams grew involved, passionate, enthusiastic, and engaged in the planning. Some of the reserve fell away once partners started planning and sharing in earnest. The enthusiasm felt in the co-planning moved mentors and mentees out of their comfort zone without creating discomfort. The pairs planned incorporating new ideas from both parties—taking risks that didn't feel so risky.

The picture-book exploration demonstrates the value of reciprocal learning in a number of ways. Foremost among these is the noticeable shift in emotion and energy that occurs when a partnership finds a positive and open communication flow. Another concrete benefit is that the natural process of creativity and revision that occurs when partners are engaged in authentic co-planning. Put another way, when our mentor pairs sat down to share ideas and resources, they brainstormed ideas ("What would happen if..."), engaged in scenario-building ("If we try this first, then..."), and relaxed enough to offer each other candid feedback in the moment ("I'm not sure if that would work because...").

A first concrete step in moving toward improved collaboration and risk-taking in classroom practice is to select and focus on a particular co-planning task, with an explicit invitation to the mentee to bring or contribute a resource. Having a third point defuses the power dynamic by creating a co-learning experience in which both parties have a chance to share their perspectives. A third point is also useful because it introduces legitimate newness into practice. That is, a mentor is creating an opportunity to bring new materials, approaches, and resources into their own classroom context. In this situation, the third point becomes additionally productive because the newness creates a positive sense of vulnerability for the mentor—which often mirrors the mentee's existing vulnerability—and helps us to become more aware of the emotional environment of the partnership.

Mentoring Move: Third Points

Focus Is Key

In response to the picture-book activity: "I like to collaborate so I thought the voices and experiences of everyone was really cool."
—Teacher Candidate, 2017

- A third point helps focus the conversation. Partnerships might draw on abstract and theoretical constructs, but the emphasis is to co-plan with students in mind.
- The strength of this Mentoring Move is that it allows for concrete discussion of a resource as it relates to diversity in the classroom. It also permits mentoring partnerships to deeply consider the strengths, interests, and needs that students present as mentor and mentee plan for a series of lessons. In this way, the process becomes a natural way for both the mentee and mentor to infuse their approach with their values, to consider inclusion and equity, and to gauge the quality of the resource they have chosen.

3 Simple Steps

1. Choose a great resource! Think about two aspects: good content and good form. That is, choose a resource that has relevant and engaging content (for example, a picture book with a social justice theme). Also, choose a resource that is not simply an excerpt from a textbook. We are partial to multimodal texts; i.e., texts that are not just print-based, but that include other modes, like images, sounds, gestures, etc. This might include picture books and graphic novels, songs, videos, field trips, guest speakers, workshops, websites, and more. A rich resource ensures a productive third point discussion.

See page 82 for the Third Points template.

2. Start a co-planning discussion, using the Third Points template on page 82. Ask questions that explore the many facets of incorporating the resource into your teaching, including differentiation and assessment.
3. Use a mindmap or web to track your discussion of the resource and co-planning.

Next Steps

- The focus of this Mentoring Move is not necessarily to enact the plan you have discussed. However, should you choose to actualize the plan, refer to Mentoring Move: Co-acting for Learning on page 41 to shape your ongoing interactions.
- This Mentoring Move can also be incorporated into school- and district-level professional development. It can be used as a follow-up to Mentoring Move: Scaling Questions (page 96) or as a stand-alone activity.

How do we negotiate difference?

Negotiating Differences

One of the inevitable questions that arises in any collaborative partnership is how to deal with differences of opinion. We propose that difference is not a negative to overcome. Rather, it is a point of potential growth and learning. The goal is to find common ground when possible, by stepping back from the situation, using a third point, or seeking mediation.

Stories from the Field: Knowing When to Hold and When to Fold (Lana)

I have served as a mentor in a half dozen contexts. Each has brought its own particular challenges and joys. These scenarios illustrate two different ways of negotiating difference.

Ally and Steven

Steven was hired into our school and Ally was assigned as his induction mentor. At the time, I was the Mentor Leader for the school, which means that I facilitated the partnerships, planned professional development sessions, and liaised with district-level contacts. Ally came to me after the first few months of school and said she needed support in her relationship with Steven. She was concerned because, in one of their conversations about assessment, Steven mentioned that he believed that only tests and exams would be suitable to evaluate mathematics learning. Ally, as one of the school's greatest champions of differentiated assessment and rich tasks in mathematics, felt particularly upset. She was worried that his students would not get the benefit of a comprehensive and participatory math program.

Chiyoung and Sylvia

Chiyoung came to me as a teacher candidate in distress. I was the Practicum Facilitator at the university, responsible for helping manage the school-university partnerships. Chiyoung voiced significant concerns about Sylvia, her mentor. She said that Sylvia maintained "a reign of terror" in her classroom, where students weren't permitted to talk or leave their desks without first raising their hands. She described how Sylvia's entire practice seemed to consist of handouts and worksheets. And finally, she mentioned tearfully that Sylvia kept making derogatory remarks about students within their earshot. Chiyoung spent a lot of time trying to refine her practice, with an emphasis on student-centred learning and a focus on equitable outcomes for all her students. She was so worried about the students that she couldn't sleep through the night.

For us, the line is clear. Negotiating difference is a natural component of any healthy mentoring relationship, especially one with a commitment to reciprocal learning. There are, however, times when a relationship is not worth preserving, when the difference is not simply predicated on different values and beliefs, but on a potentially damaging practice that threatens not only the relationship, but also the school community. Let's examine both situations a bit more closely.

Ally wanted Steven to afford his students the very latest cutting-edge pedagogy in mathematics. When Lana asked her if she had any other concerns about his teaching, his classroom management, his planning, or his instruction, Ally acknowledged that her concerns were limited to Steven's assessment practices. In our district, while there is a governing policy on assessment, a good portion of its application is based on a teacher's professional judgment. Lana's advice to Ally was to be a patient. Steven, as a newly hired teacher, was likely replicating the assessment strategies that had been modelled for him as a student. Lana suggested that she invite Steven into her classroom over the course of the year to watch her diverse assessment approaches in action: children working on rich tasks in groups at whiteboards, hands-on projects, and informal anecdotal observations. Lana suggested that, instead of problematizing Steven's assessment directly, Ally ask him about what he valued in assessment (likely rigor and validity) and how tests and exams in mathematics reflected those values. Lana also suggested that, if by year's end Steven remained steadfast in his convictions, Ally invite him to join her in a collaborative inquiry for the second year, where they could explore assessment and evaluation practice in math together.

In the case of Chiyoung and Sylvia, Lana was concerned for the students, as well as for the potential negative impact from Sylvia's model of practice. Sometimes a situation requires external intervention or even reporting. We advise mentors and mentees in this circumstance to first seek outside guidance or third-party mediation to determine appropriate next steps. Next, a decision to involve an administrator might be made if third-party mediation is not appropriate or if the safety of students has been compromised. Then, it might be necessary to dissolve the partnership, especially if one of the members has safety concerns. Finally, steps can be undertaken to support, further educate, or, in rare cases, sanction the teacher who has demonstrated the concerning behavior.

In negotiating difference, the first step is to make a decision about the nature of the difference. Look closely at the harm, if any exists. On one end of the spectrum we would ask: Are students in danger? Is administrator involvement required? On the other end of the spectrum, we would ask: Is this a point of difference worth addressing? This step helps calibrate the type of response or negotiation that may be required.

Assuming that the difference is located in the middle of the spectrum, we recommend the second step of taking a non-judgmental learning stance. Be in a place of wondering—"I wonder why this approach is important to this person" —rather than in a place of judgment—"This approach is wrong!" Give your partner some time, make observations, and ask questions. Use Mentoring Move: The Important Thing to shed light on the situation and to help build consensus.

The third step, depending on the context, is either to seek common ground or to model alternatives through practice. Look for third points to anchor the discussion; research that supports the discussion is always helpful. The third point helps shift the discussion away from "I believe" statements, which can provoke further difference and conflict, and offers outside perspective: "There are some interesting points in this research that could be useful in guiding us."

While it won't always be possible to come to an agreement on the best way to proceed, often the conversation about a difference of opinion, style, or approach can lead to better understanding, productive compromise, and improved outcomes.

Mentoring Move: The Important Thing

Consensus Is Key

"It's a really good opportunity, I think, to have that opportunity to talk with your mentor teacher and have those questions, and a good opportunity to bond with your mentor teacher."
—Teacher Candidate, 2017

- Teaching in collaboration with a mentor or mentee, or with a grade partner or lesson study colleague, requires the development of common objectives, shared understandings, and general agreement on what strategies to use and how a lesson will be implemented.
- Mentors and mentees undertake a Mentoring Move that facilitates consensus-building and collaboration as they complete statements to articulate their key ideas.

3 Simple Steps

1. Mentor and mentee identify an aspect of practice as a focus for the Mentoring Move; e.g., lesson planning, student engagement, etc. Using *The Important Book* by Margaret Wise Brown (1949) as a template, mentor and mentee complete their reflection on the important thing about an aspect of practice. Read-aloud or digital versions of the book are easily found online, where text like the following provides a clear outline for the task:

> The important thing about a spoon is that you eat with it.
> It's like a little shovel,
> You hold it in your hand,
> You can put it in your mouth,
> It isn't flat,
> It's hollow,
> And it spoons things up.
> But the important thing about a spoon is that you eat with it.

See page 83 for The Important Thing template.

2. Mentor and mentee each complete The Important Thing template on page 83, choosing a descriptor that is deemed to be the most important about the topic and continuing with several additional descriptors or attributes.
3. Mentor and mentee share their work with each other, collaborating to come to consensus on a single finished product. Mentors and mentees are encouraged to look for commonalities in the descriptors they have used, then to find overarching terms that reflect a compilation of their ideas and consensus in what is important about the topic. In some cases, mentor and mentee may negotiate a variation that prioritizes the work of one or the other. Here is an example from a group of teachers thinking about ways to engage students in learning. They shared their thoughts on the power of curiosity.

> The important thing about curiosity is that it changes me.
> It's the key that sparks thinking.
> You feel it when it engages your mind and sets it winging off in new directions.
> You can count on it to ignite learning.
> It's the basis of every question.
> And it's free!
> But the important thing about curiosity is that it changes me.

Next Steps

- Based on your experience with building consensus, work as a team to undertake an inquiry project (Mentoring Move: Inquiring Collaboratively on page 76) or the co-planning and co-teaching of a specific lesson (Mentoring Move: Co-acting for Learning on page 41).
- Consider how collaboration might enhance student learning. By giving students voice to participate in their learning and by collaborating with them to design inquiry projects, teachers support student independence in learning.
- Consider that negotiation and consensus-building will be important to the success of collaborative work throughout your career.

How might action research and inquiry facilitate mentor and mentee professional learning?

Exploring Professional Learning

No framework for reciprocal learning would be complete without some discussion of a formal and structured non-hierarchal learning process. In our section on parallel learning, we offered a strategy for becoming co-learners while maintaining separate areas of interest, learning, and research. Now we draw on the rich existing literature to suggest that action research and collaborative inquiry can provide another form of reciprocal learning for a shared area of investigation.

There is a substantial body of research that illustrates the value of teachers coming together in partnership or in small learning communities to explore a particular topic. Research reveals that there are a host of benefits of this work. When teachers come together to conduct action research or engage in collaborative inquiry, they are able to tailor inquiries in response to local communities. They can identify the greatest area of need for their school or classrooms and design an inquiry that addresses it directly.

A further benefit of teachers collaborating on research is that the work brings together diverse perspectives and voices. This is especially important for voices that are traditionally on the margins of research and policy. Put another way, collaborative inquiry and action research present grass-roots opportunities for teachers who represent or work with marginalized communities to develop a powerful voice for agency and change. The more teachers become involved in research, the more likely it is that the group will consider issues from varied perspectives, examine diverse resources, ask nontraditional questions, and experiment with emerging pedagogies.

Yet another benefit of teacher research is that it grows a sense of participatory engagement and community. Consider once again the example of the picture-book planning in our professional development session (see page 70). When people work together to achieve a common goal, it produces an energy and excitement that becomes contagious. In one of Lana's school communities, collaborative inquiry began with groups of induction mentors and mentees, but became such a point of conversation and sharing that it soon evolved into a schoolwide commitment. The possibilities for learning from one another are exponential.

And lastly, but most significantly, when teachers join in research, there are immediate, tangible benefits for students. One of the most common themes from our own research projects has been that when teachers learn, it translates into new experiences for their students. When preservice mentors for teacher candidates joined our sessions on mentoring, they provided us with direct feedback; even though the professional learning focused on mentoring, many of the strategies and tools could be adapted for the classroom. More directly, when teachers came back after a month, they told us that the results of co-planning included improved student engagement and outcomes.

The Mechanics of Action Research and Collaborative Inquiry

- **Timing:** We recommend that mentors and mentees engage in collaborative inquiry and action research after spending some time getting to know one another. One district we work with offers collaborative inquiry professional development to induction mentors and mentees in their second year, which ensures that many aspects of the relationship are already in place. Most collaborative inquiries run for at least one term or semester. The ideal would be to commit to it as a major learning focus over the course of an entire academic year.

- **Grouping:** We have found that collaborative inquiries run just as well between mentor pairs as they do in slightly larger groups of three or four. We caution against trying to run a single investigation with too large a group, because so much discussion and interaction is required. If you are working with a larger group of mentors and mentees, or with a whole-school community, we suggest that it is best when smaller groups form so that they can tailor their questions most closely to the needs of their program.
- **Structure:** As noted, there are many resources available with in-depth descriptions of process and structure for action research and collaborative inquiry. Nonetheless, we offer a graphic below that offers an overview of the flow we have used to anchor our projects.

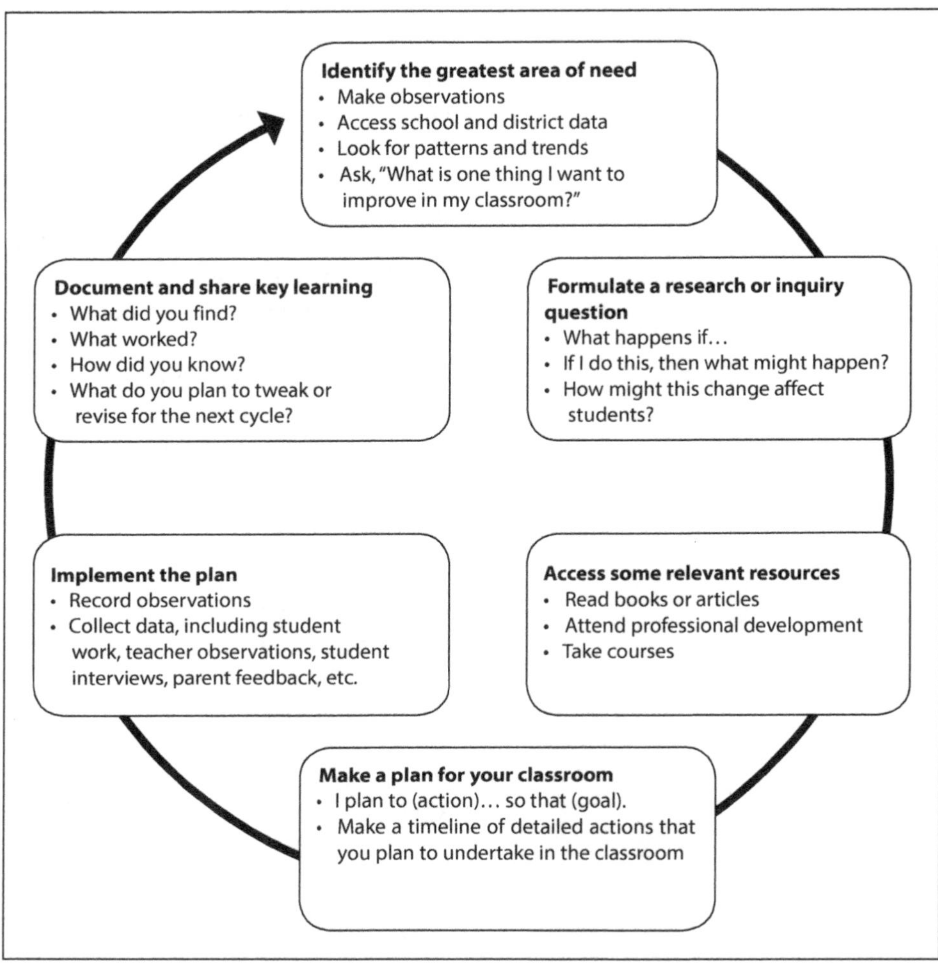

Mentoring Move: Inquiring Collaboratively

Collaboration Is Key

"It really grounds you … in terms of my teaching philosophy and theirs …and how we can build a very safe risk-taking environment."
— Mentor Teacher, 2017

- Inquiring Collaboratively facilitates an understanding that mentor and mentee optimally function as partners in the shared objective of enhancing student learning, teacher development, and the professional mentoring relationship.
- Based on concrete actions that support student learning, mentor and mentee bring the concept of experiential education to life as they implement a reciprocal model of experimentation and risk-taking pedagogy that facilitates learning and growth for both parties.

- Concrete actions for student learning within a collaborative model might include implementing the use of emerging technology in the classroom, social media as a platform for learning, or another new or developing educational trend that is of interest to both mentor and mentee.

3 Simple Steps

See page 84 for the Inquiring Collaboratively template.

1. Mentors and mentees choose a topic of mutual interest they would like to explore. This Mentoring Move is best suited to an emerging practice in education or a new technology that both partners are interested in investigating.
2. Using the Inquiring Collaboratively template on page 84, mentor and mentee act as collaborative learning partners to research and share information on the topic, then brainstorm ways to implement the learning, support each other, and collaboratively take pedagogical risks to enhance student learning.
3. Mentor and mentee conclude with an analysis of the emerging practice or technology, an assessment of student learning relevant to the new context, and reflection to enhance future implementation.

Next Steps

- Consider co-writing an article on the nature and results of the work for a professional journal or school website.
- Collaborate to prepare a professional learning workshop or after-school mini-session to share the findings.
- Use the experience as a springboard to launch an ongoing professional partnership that continues into subsequent years, or a model of partnership in learning that can result in mutual rewards for other mentoring relationships or mentoring partners in the school.
- Add the experience to your resume as an example of leadership in learning.

What I Bring

You Will Need

- A piece of chart paper
- A black marker to draw an outline of a tree on the chart paper
- Multi-colored sticky notes to represent leaves on the tree
- Pens for transcribing ideas

Instructions

1. Draw an outline of a tree on chart paper.
2. Distribute sticky notes to each mentor and mentee.
3. Invite each person to write one quality or personal characteristic that they bring to the partnership/classroom on each sticky note.
4. Place sticky notes on the tree outline.
5. Discuss the words that have been written on the sticky notes. How many of the words relate to knowledge or skills? To communication? To interpersonal skills? To values? To character?

Sharing Values, page 1

Qualities and Characteristics of a Mentor

Pembroke Publishers ©2020 *Mentoring Each Other* by Lana Parker and Diane Vetter ISBN 978-1-55138-346-0

Sharing Values, page 2

Qualities and Characteristics of a Mentee

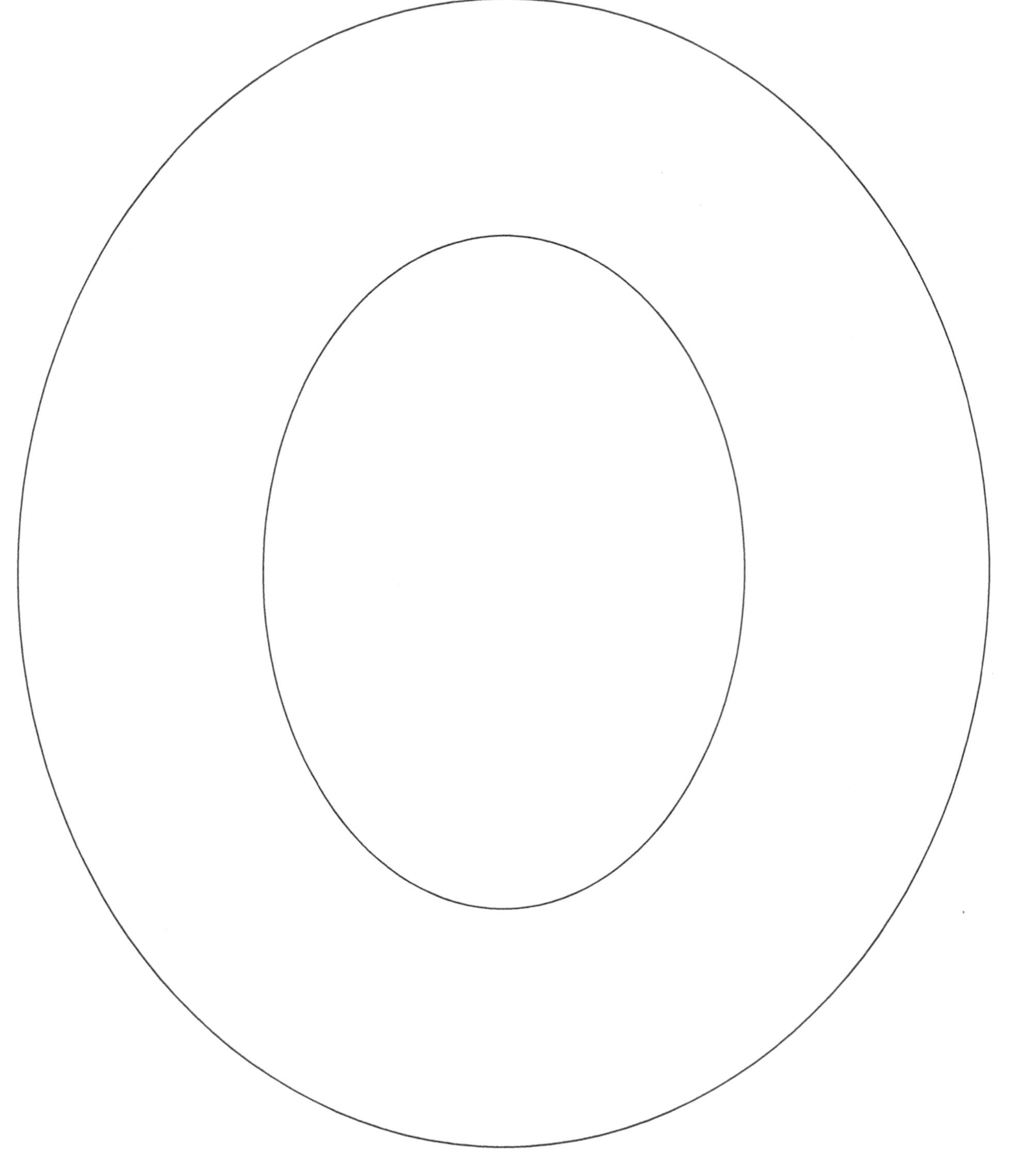

Pembroke Publishers ©2020 *Mentoring Each Other* by Lana Parker and Diane Vetter ISBN 978-1-55138-346-0

I'd Like to Learn More About...

	Mentee	Mentor
Identify: I'd like to learn more about...		
Trace: Why it is an area of interest		
Plan: Resources to use		
Plan: Strategy or tool you will try in the classroom		
Date to Report Back		

Third Points

Some questions to help get you started:

- What makes this a good resource for our students?
- What are the key ideas or themes we can explore using this resource?
- Is there anything we have to consider in advance (sensitive content, modifying for different students, etc.)?
- To what curriculum content (and to which learning goals) does this resource connect?
- How can we introduce this resource?
- What are some useful instructional strategies?
- What are some possible activities and extensions we could develop?
- How will we assess student learning?
- How can we share our learning with parents and the community?

Use a mindmap to track your questions and discussions as you co-plan.

The Important Thing

(Adapted from Wise Brown, 1994)

Use the sample on page 74 from *The Important Book* (Wise Brown, 1949) as a model to reflect on what is important relative to a specific issue. Between the opening and closing prompts, you can vary and adapt the sentence starters (*It's*, *You*, *You can*, etc.); the key is to prioritize one important aspect that opens and closes the reflection.

The important thing about _________ is...

It's...

You...

You can...

It's...

And...

But the important thing about _________ is...

Here is an example from a group of teachers thinking about ways to engage students in learning. They shared their thoughts on the power of curiosity.

The important thing about curiosity is that it changes me.
It's the key that sparks thinking.
You feel it when it engages your mind and sets it winging off in new directions.
You can count on it to ignite learning.
It's the basis of every question.
And it's free!
But the important thing about curiosity is that it changes me.

Inquiring Collaboratively

PRACTICE / ARTICLE / VIDEO / ISSUE OF INTEREST

KEY MESSAGE

A FEW DETAILS

A QUOTE THAT RESONATES

SOMETHING I CHALLENGE

QUESTIONS THAT REMAIN

IMPLICATIONS FOR PRACTICE

4

Mentoring as Leadership

In this chapter, we describe the impact of mentoring in and beyond the classroom. After spending much time working with mentors, we came to identify a relationship between mentoring and leadership in education. Through the observation of mentors' actions and interactions with mentees, we recognized that mentoring does not simply move an educator along a pathway toward leadership; mentoring *is* an act of leadership in its own right (Molitor, Parker & Vetter, 2018).

In this chapter we present a view of mentor as leader whose act of **opening the classroom door** to mentees and colleagues encourages the metacognitive processes that facilitate analysis of daily practice. We consider a physical and metaphorical space that supports mentor and mentee in achieving their desired learning outcomes, which we refer to as a **space for open minds**, where a multitude of ideas and understandings evolve and develop in new ways. We explore **communication** and **documentation for professional growth** as strategic elements to support the mentor and mentee in their learning environment. Of course, schools are communities and good work rarely remains hidden. Recognizing this, we embrace the concept of mentors as **lead learners.** We prepare mentors to think of their work as a **catalyst** for additional leadership roles in education.

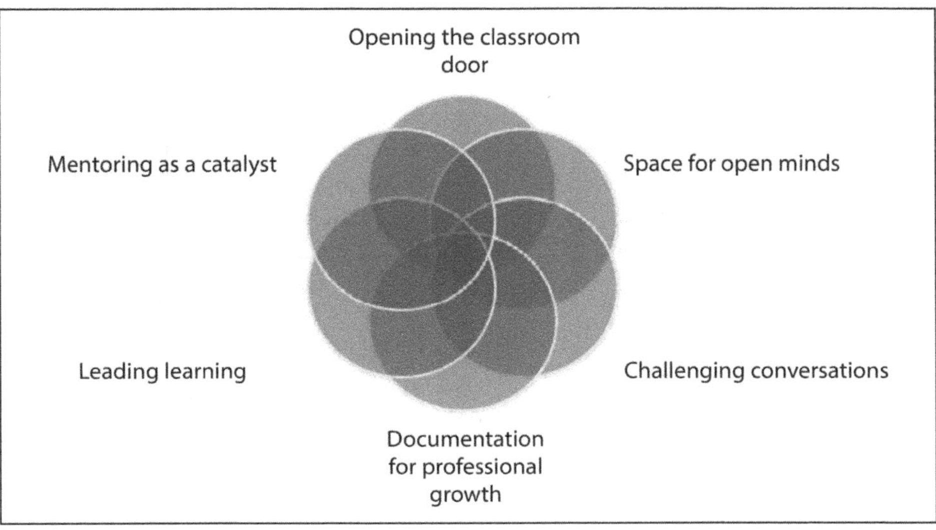

Mentors ask these key questions as they engage with the mentoring process in a leadership role:

- How might opening my classroom door demonstrate leadership? (See page 86.)
- How might I cultivate a space for open minds? (See page 89.)
- How might we navigate challenging conversations? (See page 91.)
- How might documentation for professional growth and development support leadership? (See page 94.)
- How might I lead learning? (See page 96.)
- How might mentoring serve as a catalyst for leadership in education? (See page 99.)

How might opening my classroom door demonstrate leadership?

Opening the Classroom Door

Mentoring requires us to open our classroom doors to others: to new teachers, who bring recent theoretical learnings and technologies; to colleagues, who bring the benefits of their teaching experience; and to faculties of education, who evaluate the work of a mentee through access to our classrooms and our practice. The opening or deprivatization of practice that comes with mentoring might raise some anxiety, but it also brings great rewards, as new ideas, new thinking, and new ways of being in the classroom enlighten our professional world.

It's important to acknowledge that those of us who open our doors always experience some trepidation. As authors and researchers, the acts of researching, writing, and publishing become acts of deprivatization as we share our findings and recount stories from the field. Yet, despite these feelings of vulnerability (or maybe even because of them), mentorship is a gesture of leadership. As Lieberman and Miller (2004) note, teachers demonstrate leadership when they deprivatize practice to engage in transparency and "go public" (p. 91) with their work. We hope that, in sharing our experiences as teachers, mentors, and practicum facilitators, we motivate you to recognize yourselves as leaders in education.

It is our contention that every mentor who shares their practice and opens their mind to new understandings is a leader in education. As noted in our discussion of models and mentors (see page 16), a teacher who simply models practice and presumes that a novice teacher will replicate that practice may be a good model, but is not a true mentor. Therefore, the act of leadership in mentoring is about openness. It requires both openness to sharing your practice with others and openness to deconstructing that practice, then rebuilding it in innovative ways to support professional development and student learning. Such openness can mean vulnerability to critique as well as curiosity about our practice from others. When we fully examine and analyze our pedagogies and practices, we are ready with a conscious understanding that welcomes critique and curiosity.

Stories from the Field: What if... (Diane)

When I was teaching in the elementary grades, our district moved to a four-level grading system. Students who were significantly below grade-level expectations were considered to be functioning at level one. Those slightly below grade level were level two. Those meeting the grade level expectations were level three. Those exceeding the grade level expectations were level four.

At that time, I attended a math workshop that noted that students at level one were usually able to understand *what* was happening in the learning; those in level two understood *how* it worked; those in level three knew *why* it was so; and those in level 4 could think outside the box to consider *what-if* possibilities. I soon began to apply this thinking across the curriculum. Indeed, I apply what/how/why/what-if thinking today to our work in mentoring. I encourage mentors to not simply share what they are doing in the classroom, but also to make visible how they are doing it and the rationale that underpins their work, or why they implemented the learning in that specific way. Then I ask them to reach outside the box to open their minds and their classrooms to new ways of doing as they explore what-if with mentees who might bring new ideas and ask questions that spur deeper thinking.

To apply this what/how/why/what-if philosophy to mentoring, teachers need to know themselves. They need to be able to reflect metacognitively on their learning philosophies, their practice, their fears, and their dreams to be able to reflect on the rationale they use as they undertake or eschew specific actions in the classroom. In other words, the what/how/why/what-if process is linked to metacognitive processes: how we think about our thinking, how we learn, and how we learn about our learning.

What

We believe that our foundational philosophies of education drive us to do what we do, every day, year after year. What do we hold sacred in our teaching? What philosophies are foundational to every lesson we teach and every interaction we have with students? What are our rewards, both tangible and intangible? What are the motivations that keep us focused in the middle of February when the end of the school year seems far away and we are physically and mentally exhausted? Ask yourself: *What are my motivations for taking on the role of mentor? What are my aspirations for the future? What is the most important thing about me as a teacher? What do I value most in my practice, my students, my professional abilities?*

How

The *how* in self-reflection requires us to think deeply about the practices we implement in the classroom. How do we engage our students in learning? How do we build the relationships that sustain us and our students when challenges arise? How do we make curriculum relevant, meaningful, and authentic in a fast-changing learning environment? How do we sustain our focus on achieving our objectives? Ask yourself: *How do I know that I am teaching effectively? How do I keep current the pedagogy and understandings that I need to teach successfully?*

Why

Why asks us to delve into our rationale for our practice. Why do I value this practice over another? Why is this classroom routine/assessment practice important... or is it just simply a routine? Why did students engage/disengage with today's lesson? Ask yourself: *Why does it matter to me if (insert your concern here)? Why do I lose sleep worrying about...?*

What-If

What-if allows our imaginations to run wild. Initially your what-ifs may seem like far-fetched notions, but with careful consideration and some modification, they can become plausible alternatives to support student learning. What if I totally changed the physical environment of my classroom? What if I adopted a flipped classroom (Baker, 2000) format? What if I used more/less technology? What if I embraced more talk and less writing in the classroom? What if I became the lead learner, rather than the teacher? What if I facilitated more student-led learning?

These questions are only samples. Your own questions will lead your personal metacognitive reflection on who you are as a teacher, as a mentor, and as a leader through the exploration of the what/how/why/what-if of your philosophies, fears, and future dreams. Reflecting on our role as teachers and mentors results in the development of mentor identities as leaders in our schools and in the greater education community. Mentoring deserves public recognition for the value of the work teachers do when opening their classrooms to preservice and novice teachers, and to experienced colleagues.

Mentoring Move: Opening Up Practice

Probing Is Key

"The knowledge that they have… that's so valuable. That's the reason why I'm there. I want that valuable knowledge. I don't just want to observe you."
— Teacher Candidate, 2017

- As mentors develop their practice, there are countless procedures or habits that become ingrained. This Mentoring Move asks mentor and mentee to probe classroom practices to explore the why that lies beneath the what and the how of traditional practice.
- Probing will help mentors articulate and question their philosophies and their educational practices, while mentees will have the opportunity to develop and challenge their own understandings, many of which might be based on what they observed as a child or adolescent learner.

3 Simple Steps

See page 102 for the Opening Up Practice template.

1. Mentors and mentees adopt a probing mindset as they undertake daily practice. Instead of discussing how and what, they will explore the why, the underlying rationale for daily practices and routines.
2. Using the Opening Up Practice template on page 102, mentor and mentee collaboratively probe their daily routines and practices to consider what-if. Mentors and mentees consider their practice as it serves to meet the needs of 21st-century learners, asking what might be changed or adapted and what might be validated and reinforced by viewing practices, pedagogies, and philosophies with a probative lens.
3. The end result of opening up practice is deeper understanding. The mentee moves from simply imitating the mentor to undertaking practices based on pedagogical rationale and well-considered principles. The mentor has the opportunity to probe practices in ways that may not have been previously considered to update or to affirm practice.

Next Steps

- Use ongoing probing as a form of critical thinking that asks mentors and mentees to analyze both new and traditional practices, holding them up to scrutiny against current standards and thinking.
- Turn the probing lens toward resources, texts, materials, topics, and issues that are used to support specific learning objectives. A classic novel from 1964 might continue to interest some students, but it could be rewarding to consider other current works that have been written in the intervening years and are

worthy of literary attention. Is everyone in the class reading the same novel? If so, what is the rationale?

- Ensure that probing is done with sincere intent. The objective is not to cast aside or challenge every aspect of pedagogy. Rather, the purpose is to avoid practicing by rote, and to embrace practice based on rationale that makes defensible sense to the professional educator.

How might I cultivate a space for open minds?

Making Space for Open Minds

In this section, we investigate listening and being together in time and space as the central process involved in mentoring work. Based on our research, we have built an argument for listening that welcomes unplanned outcomes and makes space for vulnerability. We refer to this as a *space for open minds*. While we have spent considerable time preparing ourselves for an open mind through reciprocal learning (see Chapter 3), we also need to consider physical space. This space might be busy or serene, brightly colored or neutral in hue. It might be brimming with visual stimuli or sparsely decorated. Regardless of the physical nature of the space, a space for open minds conveys the message, "You are welcome here." The space mirrors the faces in the classroom and ensures that everyone feels that they are known and respected.

Stories from the Field: The View from My Window (Diane)

One of my fondest memories from teaching in elementary schools comes from a school in a rural town. My classroom faced the parking lot. Between our window and the parking lot was a hardscrabble patch of dirt with big tree in the middle. There was some litter and a few weeds that dared to peek up through the hard earth. For a couple of years, I looked out at that dirt and wished for a nicer view, but funds were tight and any fundraising went to a breakfast program for hungry kids or books for the library.

One day I mentioned to a colleague, who shared a similar parking lot/dirt view, that it would be nice to look out on some green space, to gather the kids around the tree to read a book in the nice weather. Chatting to a few other teachers, the idea took flight. We couldn't afford landscape fabric, so we collected old newspapers that the Kindergarten students spread over the hard dirt. The Grade 7 and 8 kids spread topsoil that was donated by a local nursery. Some parents donated plants that the primary and junior students planted in our new garden. My colleague's dad built a bench around the tree. On the day we put it all together, my class ran a drive-through window, serving cold water and juice to those whose turn it was to contribute their labor to the garden.

It was certainly wonderful to look out our classroom window to see plants growing and a tree with a bench where we could sit and read. However, the best part of the project was the spirit that it created. Our view reminded us daily that everyone (Kindergarten kids to teens, parents, and teachers) could achieve so much when we opened our minds to possibilities. This open-minded perspective led us to consider alternative ways of learning. One day we spent most of the day researching spiders and tracking the growing web that was forming outside our window. We raised butterflies in the classroom and released them in our garden. When we changed our view, we also changed our perspectives on what we could do and what it meant to be a community of learners.

A space for open minds is a not about square footage. It is about representation of relationships, possibilities, shared values, multiple perspectives, and willingness to open up to new ideas.

Imagine that you could buy and sell a classroom in the same way that you buy and sell a house. What would a buyer see, walking in the door of your classroom? Is there a feeling of welcome and warmth that would make someone want to buy it for their students? Does it feel like a safe haven in a busy world? Are the faces of the occupants reflected in the space, or is it somewhat impersonal? Is the space an inclusive environment where all feel comfortable, or do some seem to have their noses to the glass, peering into a space that seems out of alignment with their reality? Do the books on the shelves represent the students and staff who inhabit your classroom? Do those books say, "You belong here"? Is there space for a newcomer to move right in, feel at home, and claim a little patch to call their own?

Mentoring Move: A Space for Open Minds

Open Minds Are Key

"It was a positive experience where my mentor teacher and I could bond, discuss our goals, and have a safe space to ask questions sometimes not considered in the classroom."
— Teacher Candidate, 2017

- A reality of the mentor/mentee relationship is that it often takes place within the mentor's environment. The unfamiliarity that the mentee feels in the mentor's physical space can be representative of the mentee's comfort level with the intellectual, social, and emotional environment of the workplace.
- A learning space for open minds shared by mentor and mentee allows knowledge, ideas, ways of knowing, and experiences to come together in an open and inclusive manner that facilitates communication, sharing of ideas and philosophies, and respect for differing perspectives and experiences.

3 Simple Steps

See page 103 for the A Space for Open Minds template.

1. Mentors and mentees acknowledge and respect their differences as individuals and as teachers, recognizing that the building of the relationship is enhanced by the concept of a learning space for open minds. Using the A Space for Open Minds template on page 103, consider what this space looks like, feels like, and sounds like.
2. Ensure the mentee has a physical space to call their own, perhaps a small corner of the classroom beside a bulletin board that the mentee can use to represent their unique place in the overall space. Quick chats could then happen at the mentee's space or the mentor's, rather than always at the mentor's desk.
3. For longer conversations, choose meeting spaces that are quiet, are private, and permit open conversation that will not be overheard or evaluated by others. Allow the neutrality of the physical space to symbolize the safety and positivity of the intellectual, social, and emotional space within which conversations will take place.

Next Steps

- Think about how *discourse* or education jargon (Gee, 2004) might affect the neutrality of a space. Are you using language or terminology that is unfamiliar to the other, creating discomfort and dominating the space?
- Be aware of your body language and facial expression. Does your posture and the look on your face reinforce or negate the intended openness of the conversation? Are you relaxed in the chair as the conversation unfolds or are you poised on the edge of your seat, ready to escape?

- Be fully present and ready to learn in the learning space for open minds. Focus on the other person with respect and patience as they share their thoughts.

How might we navigate challenging conversations?

Challenging Conversations

For most of us, challenging conversations are the most difficult part of mentoring. As teachers, we tend to be nurturers, striving to inspire and motivate our students. Managing challenging conversations that often result from conflict are never pleasant. This section provides strategies and conversation starters to support mentors in engaging in those challenging conversations.

Let's consider the background that makes those conversations difficult. In discussions with our colleagues in other fields that require practicum experiences (nursing, social work, healthcare), we know that evaluating practical experiences is a shared concern. Mentees who are able to accept a low academic course grade with logical reasoning (e.g., "I could have studied harder," "I didn't dedicate enough time and/or effort," or "I misread the expectations") often regard an unsuccessful practicum or internship experience as a personal failure that diminishes their confidence and self-esteem. Perhaps, as teachers, we also harbor this divided understanding when evaluating practical experiences. While it might not be easy to assign a low grade to student assignments or exams, we do so based on criteria that allow us to frame our decision. We realize that we are evaluating student work, rather than evaluating the student as a person. Yet in evaluating practicum performance, the line seems to blur. Perhaps we, too, struggle to articulate explicit feedback on practical experience for fear that it might have a negative impact on a mentee's self-esteem or erode their confidence. When we factor in that many struggling mentees have come to the mentoring partnership already demonstrating low levels of confidence and/or anxiety, providing explicit feedback on gaps and unsuccessful practice becomes exceedingly difficult.

Stories from the Field: Refocusing Frustration (Diane)

I recall a teacher candidate arriving in my office angry and in tears. Lee was sure that her mentor hated her. She had a long list of evidence as to why she felt persecuted, along with a lengthy defence to rebut the concerns that the mentor had raised about Lee's practice. The elevated pitch and accelerated pace of Lee's voice made clear her agitation.

My first step was simply to listen attentively to Lee's message and the emotions that accompanied its delivery. I made sure to maintain eye contact and lean forward in my chair a bit to ensure my body language and my facial expression demonstrated that Lee's message was being heard and carefully considered. When Lee finished speaking, I allowed for an extended pause to let her catch her breath and prepare to focus on what I had to say. My pitch and pace were deliberately lower and slower to de-escalate the tension that lingered in the air and was only slowly dissipating. I did not specifically address the evidence that Lee had presented, so as not to enter into a true/false discussion. Rather I began by explaining to Lee that in every mentor/mentee relationship professionalism is of primary importance. I asked her to pause for a moment and think about how she might have managed the relationship with the mentor-teacher differently. Neither of us could control or change the past, so I headed to the heart of the matter: how to move forward in a professional manner. I asked her to identify two concrete and specific things she could or would do differently in the same situation, and how those actions might have had a positive impact on the situation we were now facing. As Lee began to consider positive actions she might take or have taken, the blame for the breakdown in the mentor/mentee relationship slowly retreated. It was no longer a conversation about a difficult history; rather, it was a conversation about opportunities to approach issues in a different way. We spoke about the importance of collegiality in professional relationships and Lee thought of ways she might have presented her ideas or concerns, and ways she might have heard her mentor's ideas and concerns, without conflict.

When Lee emailed me the following evening, after having spent the day with her mentor in the classroom, she was very optimistic that things were going to turn around in her placement. She shared that she and her mentor had agreed that much of the conflict was due to miscommunication, and that they both shared the same goal of a successful practicum experience for Lee and successful learning for the students in the classroom. The mentor and mentee had agreed to share a focus on facilitating successful student learning. They also agreed that successful student learning required thoughtful planning and organization. Shifting the focus to successful student learning meant that Lee was taking initiative and responsibility for effective planning and organization—the two issues in Lee's prior practice that had been of concern to the mentor—not because the mentor was consistently reminding her to do so, but as a response to the shared goal of successful student learning.

The objective in a challenging conversation is to create and focus on a shared objective that both parties willingly align their actions to achieve. The goal is never to make a point or convince someone of something. Such objectives do not result in resolutions, only short-term respites from conflict until the issues manifest once again. A focus on shared objectives depersonalizes the issues and opens minds to a solution to which all parties can contribute, even if those contributions come from different places or perspectives.

In some cases, we have the opportunity to plan for a challenging conversation. Other times, issues arrive on our doorstep without warning. In either case, professionalism is key. If you have the opportunity to plan for a challenging conversation, schedule a time when stress levels are low. The end of a hectic day when everyone is tired and stressed is not a good time. If you must meet at the end of the day, allow time for a cup of tea, a few good deep breaths, or quiet reflection before the conversation is scheduled to begin. Arrive in a calm rather than flustered state.

If a challenging conversation lands unexpectedly on your doorstep, allow the person who has initiated the conversation plenty of time to present their concerns while you listen attentively. Do not interrupt the speaker. Begin the challenging conversation only when the speaker has finished explaining their concerns. At that time, you can ask for clarification of anything you did not understand before proceeding with the next step.

In all challenging conversations, remember these simple guidelines:

- *Professionalism is key.* Maintain a professional and collegial stance. Your purpose is to collaboratively resolve an issue through the establishment of a shared objective, rather than to provide a solution or "fix" for the problem.

- *Allow the other person to have their say.* People need the opportunity to be heard without interruption or implied judgment in your demeanor.
- *Maintain a calm manner.* Ensure the pace and pitch of your voice support a calm conversation. Avoid confrontational statements, accusations, or defensive postures.
- *Recognize the power of silence.* If the conversation becomes heated, take a pause. Provide a silent space to allow for a return to a professional and collegial conversation.
- *Focus on shared objectives.* Once the speaker has had their voice heard, do not rehash past history. Discuss or brainstorm concrete and specific actions that will resolve the issue, allowing the other person to take initiative and responsibility for creating positive actions and next steps.

After the challenging conversation has ended, make time to sum up the meeting with an email briefly summarizing the concern, the shared objective, positive actions, and next steps. If issues arise again, the email is a great reference back to what "we agreed upon."

Mentoring Move: Wondering

Wondering Is Key

"I have a plan... there's a purpose now. I can go, 'Am I being too evasive?'"
— Mentor Teacher, 2017

- This Mentoring Move asks both mentor and mentee to avoid a judgmental stance and "turn to wonder" (Palmer, 2007) when expectations are not met or outcomes are below standard. In the midst of a busy day or a stress-filled week, patience can be low and disappointment or frustration might be evident. Turning to wonder allows mentors and mentees to consider why rather than fixate on the what.
- Using the Wondering template on page 104, mentors and mentees are encouraged to explore the underlying causes of instructional challenges and implement meaningful strategies to address issues or concerns with a view to improving future practice.

3 Simple Steps

See page 104 for the Wondering template.

1. Review the Wondering template on page 104 to consider questions or statements that encourage wonder and support a partner in finding their own resolution to an issue, instead of expecting someone else to provide a ready-made solution.
2. Make a commitment to wonder rather than rush to judgment if frustrations arise in the relationship. Commit to asking thoughtful questions to help a partner to understand the root of a problem and uncover ways to address issues.
3. End with a commitment to use the understanding developed to implement next steps. For example, a mentor might commit to being more explicit with explanations of expectations, while a mentee might commit to thinking more deeply about what needs to be done to meet the expectations before rushing into the task.

Next Steps

- Honor the lived experiences of both mentor and mentee, understanding that the norms that are foundational to our expectations might not be the same as those for someone whose experience and way of being in the world differs from our own. For example, differences in background, culture, and generation can greatly affect tacit norms.

- Always ask yourself how your perception of a situation might differ from that of your mentor or mentee before addressing an issue or concern.
- Look deeply within to analyze how your actions or words, or lack thereof, might have resulted in a miscommunication or a differing understanding of expectations.

How might documentation for professional growth and development support leadership?

Documentation for Professional Growth

As we begin this conversation about documentation, it is important to clarify our foundational belief. We believe that teachers are professionals who take responsibility for their ongoing professional learning throughout their careers. With independence in their daily practice, they are their own best evaluators. As professionals, teachers take responsibility for identifying gaps in understandings or challenges in practice and seek ways to implement change. For some, this might mean taking professional learning courses; others might seek the support of a colleague as mentor. Some undertake independent research or study, while others seek out colleagues to form an inquiry group or professional learning community to share in the exploration of the issues they face in their practice.

Given this professional disposition toward independent self-reflection and collegial or independent learning to address knowledge gaps and issues, we believe it is important to establish the practice of self-assessment early in the process of learning about teaching. A mentor needs to demonstrate how to engage in ongoing reflective self-assessment (see Mentoring Move: Stoplight Self-Assessment on page 50). To support this process, we suggest that both mentors and mentees retain *documented evidence* to help them look objectively at their practice. For mentors who aspire to other opportunities for leadership in education, documentation of successes achieved and challenges met provides solid evidence of a mentor's readiness to take on additional leadership roles. In addition, both mentors and mentees who undertake a collection of documented evidence and use it to inform their practice will establish a habit of taking responsibility for their own professional development and demonstrate initiative in leading their own learning.

A collection of documented evidence can be retained, refreshed, or discarded and restarted each year; however, the practice of seeking evidence that indicates success or challenges in daily practice is one that we highly recommend. Unlike a traditional portfolio that a teacher might retain for interview purposes or to support performance appraisals, a collection of documented evidence becomes a practical tool for self-assessment, as well as a showcase. It also becomes a history of learning and a testament to experience that encourages the transference of success when a new challenge arises.

Stories from the Field: Tell Me About... (Diane)

I was working with a mentor who was supporting a struggling novice teacher. The mentor had experienced much prior success with other mentees, but this particular mentoring relationship was not going well. The mentor was feeling discouraged and taking the blame for what she saw as a failure in her mentoring.

After listening to the details of the situation, I asked the mentor to recount some of the success stories from prior mentoring experiences. As the stories began to unfold, the mentor became energized and was able to pick out strategies and supports that had been successful with previous mentees and might be applied in this situation. She soon came to recognize that she was a successful mentor and that she had the experience and mentoring skills to work through this situation.

The mentor later got back to me to say that the situation had turned around and things were going well. She also noted that she had used my strategy with her mentee. She had asked the mentee to tell her about a lesson where he felt the students were really engaged in the learning. Then she asked, "How might you have re-created that engagement in today's lesson? What did you do differently in the prior lesson? What have you discovered that you might apply to future lessons?" When you are coming from a place of prior success, documented evidence can be very motivating by keeping the focus on the demonstrated ability to succeed, while still addressing current challenges.

Leadership is not about having all the answers. It is about facilitating growth and success in others. Leadership is also about being able to look at documentation and dig beneath the surface to help others move ahead.

Stories from the Field: Standardized Testing (Diane)

I was working with a school whose scores on standardized testing were low. Teachers and parents spoke about the limitations of using standardized tests and their scores as a gauge of learning, but that didn't alter the perception that the school was somehow failing. In addition, the district's test scores were publicized, so the results were public knowledge. Even the students were affected, with many making self-deprecating jokes to cover up the fact that their school had not fared well.

Our perspectives changed, however, when we took the test data and, rather than comparing it to other schools, compared it to the previous years' data for the same school. Surprise! The data showed an improvement in the school's score from previous years, and the number of students in the lowest ranking had dropped dramatically. The interpretation of the data with a different lens changed how we felt about the results.

We send our appreciation to Jim Strachan, an amazing educator in Ontario who introduced us to scaling questions.

Documented evidence is not simply about recording varying levels of success. It also provides witness to growth and development. The next Mentoring Move is a documentation strategy that we use with mentors and mentees to turn the spotlight on improvement. Thinking of making minor modifications for improvement seems much less onerous than reworking a whole lesson, project, or initiative. In addition, when that one modification is successfully made, it becomes a good motivator to continue implementing the Scaling Questions strategy to see small but steady and consistent improvement.

Mentoring Move: Scaling Questions

"Sometimes we're thrown in situations where we feel like we have to come up with something on the spot. And that's super intimidating."
— Teacher Candidate, 2017

Analysis Is Key

- Scaling questions facilitate self-analysis of practice, giving ownership of the reflection and subsequent planning process to the individual who wishes to improve practice or address a concern. Rather than relying on the opinion or evaluation of another, scaling questions support the independent appraisal of practice that will be required of an educator on an ongoing basis.
- The objective of this Mentoring Move is to reduce the stress of the evaluation process and to foster independence and analytical practice. The reflection process can be facilitated by a mentoring partner, but the actual analysis remains the work of the individual who owns the practice or concern.

3 Simple Steps

See page 105 for the Scaling Questions template.

1. Using the Scaling Questions template on page 105, rate a specific lesson or practice on a scale of 1 to 10. Provide rationale for the decision and contemplate how that rating might be increased by simply one point (in reference to practice) or decreased simply by one point (in reference to the impact of a concern).
2. The mentoring partner will act as a sounding board in the process, asking open questions that support deeper probing into the analysis.
3. End with an action plan detailing how the lesson or practice might be improved if it were to be taught again. Consider alternative strategies, resources, or timings that might have made the lesson more successful. Consider how the physical environment contributed to the success of the lesson or created challenges. Were the needs of all students considered? How might student engagement have supported or disrupted the learning? Asking these questions helps to dig deeply and improve practice.

Next Steps

- In analyzing the practice, it is important to look holistically at a lesson to determine an overall rating, rather than judge the whole lesson based on one aspect that may or may not have been successful.
- Consider using this strategy with students in the classroom to help them develop their assessment skills and improve their work and their learning. This initial step into metacognitive thinking will be of great value to students at all grade levels and to teachers of varying experience.
- Remember that the goal of scaling questions is not to generate immediate leaps, but rather to identify small concrete steps that can be consistently undertaken to improve practice.

How might I lead learning?

Leading Learning

Like mentoring, leadership is not about perfection. Indeed, it is about having the courage and the grace to open your practice and beliefs in education to the scrutiny of your peers—both novice and experienced. It is about retaining and sharing that sense of wonder and enthusiasm for learning that led you to this profession. It is about understanding that not knowing is an opportunity to become curious.

Stories from the Field: Don't Fake It 'til you Make It (Diane)

I recall having to teach a science unit on electricity to my Grade 5 class. I had just moved to Grade 5 from the primary division and, to be honest, I didn't know much about electricity. So I read the text book and quizzed my elderly father, who wondered why, after 40 years, he was still helping me with my homework. I was quite prepared to head into the classroom with a fake-it-'til-you-make-it attitude. Then I reconsidered. What if I admitted to the class that I knew little about electricity? What if I modelled for them how to learn something new? What if I let those kids who knew more teach me about electricity?

So I packed up my hairdryer and went to school. I stood at the front of the class, turned on the hairdryer, and aimed it toward my hair. The class looked at me a bit askance and questioned what I was doing. I told them that I was sharing pretty much everything that I knew about electricity: that if I plug in my hair dryer, current makes it work. I admitted that I wasn't 100% sure of how the current got from Niagara Falls to my hair dryer.

It turned out to be an amazing collaborative learning experience. As leader in the learning, I was able to demonstrate how to research, how to identify gaps in my learning, and how to think critically about information I discovered. Setting aside the role of *knower* to become *not knower* totally changed the dynamic in our classroom and led to new and innovative ways of learning.

The point of this narrative is that all of us can be leaders in learning. A true leader is not necessarily the most brilliant or the most knowledgeable, or even the most experienced. True leadership is a mindset that is open to listening and embraces both the power and the vulnerability of not knowing, creating a catalyst that drives transformation and new opportunities for learning and instructional leadership.

As lead learner, a mentor can take on the role of curator, helping a mentee access resources, information, and research relative to a given topic. Particularly in today's information age, a mentor's key task as a lead learner might be to support identification of what is relevant, factual, and useful to the shared learning. While an Internet search can yield a long list of articles, websites, and resources, it is important to know that what is presented to you in your search of a specific topic or key word might differ from what is presented to another Internet user. Search results are selected for users based on prior searches. What your search window reveals could reflect only your specific interest or lens on an issue, as determined by the search engine.

To yield information that provides multiple perspectives on a topic or issue, it is important to dig deeper and seek out research and information that provides alternate perspectives and challenges your current understandings. Lead learners need to look at resources with the same critical lens that they encourage their students to use in the classroom, asking the following:

- How is the language in the resource attempting to manipulate my stance on the topic, or presuppose authority or power?
- What assumptions does the author make?
- Whose voices are present or missing in the presentation of the text?
- Who is advantaged/disadvantaged by the research?
- How is this research relevant or applicable to our environment?

- What is missing from the data? (Remember the Standardized Testing story on page 95 about data that told a partial and imperfect story.)
- How might we assess the reliability, validity, and credibility of the data presented?

In their classrooms, with their mentees, and within professional learning communities, mentors have the experience, the expertise, and the opportunity to become highly effective lead learners.

A final thought about leading learning: As we are teachers, much of our experience with leadership may have come from hierarchical relationships where the leader has authority to make decisions or impose policy. In a professional learning context, leading the learning comes from a collaborative stance that does not impose prior notions nor set out to prove a point of view. Leading the learning is an open-minded exploration of possibilities that begins with curiosity and leads to new ways of being that ultimately enhance the education experience.

Mentoring Move: A Critical Lens

Critical Thinking Is Key

"Most valuable… learning the different perspectives of the education system."
— Teacher Candidate, 2017

- Giroux (1994) challenges teachers to make schools into places of "critical education in the service of creating a public sphere of citizens who are able to exercise power over their own lives and especially over the conditions of knowledge acquisition" (p. 41).
- Whether we are taking on the role of lead learners as classroom teachers working with students, as mentors working with novice or experienced teachers, or as colleagues collaborating on inquiry-based practiced, the ability to exercise power over our knowledge acquisition is central to the learning objective.

3 Simple Steps

See page 106 for the A Critical Lens template.

1. Using the A Critical Lens template on page 106, share a practice that you implement in your classroom to support critical thinking amongst your students.
2. Apply the practice to the information, resources, or knowledge that you will access as lead learner within a collaborative learning project and record on the template under Impact on Process.
3. Discuss with colleagues or mentees how the practice of critical thinking has impact on the collaborative process that you are undertaking and how it might affect the outcome of your work. In other words, how might the critical thinking practice that you undertake facilitate the exercising of power over the conditions of your collaborative knowledge acquisition? Record on the template under Impact on Outcome.

Next Steps

- As educators who apply a critical lens to our own professional inquiries, consider how this thinking might influence mentor/mentee and student/teacher relationships.
- Consider how the value of critical power is seriously diminished when opportunities to implement change as a result of critical thinking are limited. In what ways might educators lead the learning that facilitates change and transformation in education practice and policy?

How might mentoring serve as a catalyst for additional leadership roles in education?

Mentoring as a Catalyst for Leadership

When we talk about leadership in education, first thoughts often go to those who choose a formal leadership trajectory as in-school curriculum leads, department heads, administrators, district leaders, and policy makers. As we have previously acknowledged, we believe that mentors are leaders whose skills in working with colleagues and openness to sharing their practice demonstrate leadership in education. Mentoring does not simply serve as a pathway to leadership. It *is* leadership that opens doors to both formal and informal leadership roles.

In some local districts, teachers with five or more years of experience and requisite academic qualifications can apply for a position as a school administrator. Following the British model, administrators were once called *head teachers*, with their role as instructional leaders clearly defined in the title. In the mid-19th century, the term *principal teacher* (later *principal*) described the person who was the principal or lead teacher in the school and the administrative liaison to centralized school districts. Today, the term *administrator* has become more common and the administrative responsibilities more time-consuming.

Stories from the Field: My Dreadful Day (Diane)

In our school, the number of students did not merit the assignment of a vice-principal or assistant administrator. If the principal were to be absent from the school, a teacher was assigned to cover the duties and a supply or occasional teacher was assigned to cover that teacher's classes. On the day I was assigned to cover for the principal, a groundhog was stuck under the fence in our schoolyard. A schoolyard full of children at recess did not help with the caretaker's rescue attempt. The animal would viciously attack the shovel when it approached to widen the exit hole; local animal control in our small town were on another call; and I spent the whole morning dealing with worried children, concerned parents, school-board maintenance personnel, and teachers who wanted the whole thing resolved as it was a distraction to the day's lessons. Added to that, the milk delivery didn't arrive for lunch and an irate community member wanted to know why the school was discarding the set of encyclopedias that had been purchased with parent-committee funding. I hoped I was diplomatic in sharing that much of the information in those encyclopedias was at best outdated, and in many cases inaccurate, after 25 years on our library shelves.

That was the day I decided that, for me, any aspirations of a formal leadership role in education would not mean taking on an administrative role. It set me on a path to consider how I might serve the education community beyond my classroom in other ways.

In the school environment, where formal leadership hours might be consumed by a myriad of competing issues, instructional leadership might also come from other school-based sources. Today, many administrators will admit to the challenge of finding time for instructional leadership within a demanding administrative portfolio that includes responsibility for school operations and staffing. Consequently, less-formalized instructional leadership, such as mentoring colleagues, including novice or preservice teachers, and engaging with professional learning communities (PLCs) that facilitate independent inquiry, have become the norm in many districts. Mentor teachers are well prepared to take on this instructional leadership role, with strong academic understandings, rich practical experience, and a sincere desire to nurture colleagues in today's and tomorrow's classrooms.

Many of the teachers who apply to teach methods courses at faculties of education are mentors. They bring a unique lens to teacher education, having rich classroom experience, coupled with an understanding of the challenges preservice teachers face in a 21st-century classroom. As researchers, our career trajectories began with classroom teaching. We then assumed mentoring roles in schools and districts, before moving to positions with faculties of education.

Within schools or across districts, instructional leadership can also take the form of collaborative learning through Professional Learning Communities (PLCs) or, as we discuss in Chapter 5, mentoring communities. These groups provide unique opportunities for mentor teachers to share their ideas, their curiosity, and their research to facilitate ongoing professional learning. Mentors who embrace the reciprocity of learning with colleagues, mentees, and students in their classrooms are well-positioned to participate in and lead the learning in the greater education community.

Mentoring Move: Tomorrow's Leaders

Vision Is Key

"It made me for sure a better teacher. He's coming in today. I better have my stuff ready. His questions make me think, 'Yeah why do I do that?' After this experience I am a way better teacher."
— Mentor Teacher, 2017

Mentoring is leadership. Yet many mentors have never previously thought of themselves as mentors or leaders. Mentors, particularly in a preservice education context, might see themselves simply as "hosts" to an upcoming colleague. Other mentors might see their mentoring roles as a first step in a leadership path toward traditional positions of responsibility or teacher education. While yet others see mentoring as a unique form of professional development that improves their practice. Many mentees will later decide to go on to mentor others, based on the strength of the mentoring relationship that they enjoyed when they began their careers. Regardless of the reason for mentoring, the profession depends on strong mentors who have a vision for what good mentoring looks like and are willing to make an effort to hone their mentoring skills.

3 Simple Steps

See page 107 for the Tomorrow's Leaders template.

1. Use the prompts provided on the Tomorrow's Leaders template on page 107 to personalize a mentoring vision to meet the needs of both mentor and mentee.
2. Consider the key elements of relational trust (see Mentoring Move: Relational Trust on page 24) and work through an analysis of your areas for personal growth. Where might mentor and mentee grow together or support the growth of the other?
3. Begin with the future in mind. Use the template as a guide to determine your short-term objectives and long-term goals for this mentoring relationship. How will this mentoring relationship make a positive impact on the future practice of mentor and mentee? How might mentor and mentee influence the greater mentoring community in the school and/or the profession?

Next Steps

- Seek out mentoring workshops or courses to develop your mentoring skills.
- Think about how the Mentoring Moves recommended for use with mentees could be easily adapted to support your work with students in your classroom.

- Connect with teacher educators in your local area to determine if a session on mentoring might be offered in your school or district as a professional learning session.
- Consider implementing mentoring strategies within your school as part of a professional or collaborative learning community.
- Start a mentoring movement in your school so that mentors and mentees can get to know each other and provide collegial peer support.

Opening Up Practice

Make a list of one or two current practices, pedagogies, or philosophies that are present in your daily classroom routine. List them in the What column.

Examine critically the practices, pedagogies or philosophies in the first column to explore What-If thinking.

What	What-If

Pembroke Publishers ©2020 *Mentoring Each Other* by Lana Parker and Diane Vetter ISBN 978-1-55138-346-0

A Space for Open Minds

Allow this circle to represent the space for open minds in your classroom. Fill the space with words that represent your vision of what the space looks like, feels like, and sounds like. Then think of ways, even small changes, that might represent the first steps to making it happen.

Pembroke Publishers ©2020 *Mentoring Each Other* by Lana Parker and Diane Vetter ISBN 978-1-55138-346-0

Wondering

Non-Judgmental Question Tips

- Quote what the speaker said then ask for clarification, instead of paraphrasing with your interpretation of the issue.
- Ask questions to which you do NOT know the answer. Avoid framing advice as a question such as, "Don't you think it might be a good idea to…". Or, "Have you ever thought of…"
- Take time to phrase your question carefully, while feeling comfortable in allowing space for silence.

Sample Questions

What are some things you find most challenging?

What did you learn from this scenario?

What surprised you as you described your scenario?

How are you feeling about this scenario now that you have articulated your thoughts?

What assumptions have you made in this scenario?

How might you look at this scenario with an alternate lens?

Where do you see hope?

What do you continue to wonder?

Scaling Questions

Scaling questions originated in the counselling profession to facilitate self-constructed solutions of issues or concerns (de Shazer, 1994).

My rating of this practice or concern is

1 2 3 4 5 6 7 8 9 10

My rationale for choosing this rating is...

____

____

____

I can improve my practice or lessen my concern by ONE STEP on the rating scale by implementing the following changes:

- ____
  ____
- ____
  ____
- ____
  ____

A Critical Lens

Critical Practice	Impact on Process	Impact on Outcome

Create a word web of concrete actions that a lead learner or a mentor might undertake to facilitate a spirit of critical engagement within the process of collaborative learning.

Tomorrow's Leaders

The strength of our partnership is ____.

A challenge we face in our partnership is ______________________________________.

To develop our partnership, we are focusing on __________________________________.

Three words I would use to describe our partnership are

____

____

____

Our short-term objectives (measurable steps) are

____

____

____

Our long-term goals are

____

____

____

Pembroke Publishers ©2020 *Mentoring Each Other* by Lana Parker and Diane Vetter ISBN 978-1-55138-346-0

5

Creating Mentoring Communities

The word *mentoring* brings to mind dyads: two people working in partnership to share knowledge and achieve some mutual objectives. For us, this image of mentoring has always seemed a bit limited by the confines of a two-person relationship, even if that is the convention. For that reason, our research not only sought to engage mentor pairs in reciprocal learning, but also to create conditions where a community of mentors and mentees could emerge. In bringing groups of mentors together to share their individual narratives and challenges, we designed professional learning that included both preservice and induction mentors, who helped us to understand that mentoring—like much teaching—can be a lonely task. Mentors told us, in surveys and focus groups, that being together for the first time had facilitated knowledge growth and had also fostered new connections within and among schools. Next, we brought the mentees into the professional learning communities with their mentors. Within this learning environment, we observed them forging stronger relationships and asking different questions.

Through the years of research, we discovered that one of the greatest (and mostly untapped) learning opportunities was to bring these previously dyadic partnerships into communities of learning and practice. But a mentoring community does not just happen. It requires intention, planning, leadership, and support. When you add that to the demands of an already busy workload, fostering a mentoring community might seem like yet another layer of work. But we are convinced that the effort pays large and powerful dividends.

We believe that there is something unique about the way a mentoring relationship can deepen learning. For this reason, we advocate that educators look for ways to extend mentoring relationships beyond the traditional dyad. Mentoring communities are powerful centres for learning, relationship-building, pedagogical exploration, and deep reflection. They offer us insight into ourselves as individual mentors and educators, and they reveal how we make connections with others. Finally, and perhaps most powerfully, mentoring communities lessen feelings of isolation by bringing educators together to form new networks. These networks become the foundation for teacher retention, wellbeing, and career longevity.

Therefore, in this final chapter, we explore the fullest expression of mentoring potential: the creation of mentoring communities that bring groups together in dynamic opportunities for sharing, listening, and learning. We begin by offering what we hope is a very compelling **rationale for mentoring** communities that overcomes some of the reluctance that may be felt by those already stretched in their responsibilities. We consider how to go about **fostering a mentoring community** when starting as an individual mentor, district coach, or administrator. Once the stage is set for a community to come together, we suggest that one of the most effective tools at our disposal is **sharing stories** to make connections, encounter different perspectives, and identify common challenges. Among the benefits of mentoring communities is the possibility to affect change that grows exponentially, and the impact of mentoring communities is, at least, threefold. The first of these impacts is the change that takes place within the traditional dyad as that partnership **witnesses others in action**. The second possible impact comes as the group develops the ability to **advance school and system goals**. And the third impact is the one that has the most potential: the opportunity to **adapt learning about mentoring to the classroom**.

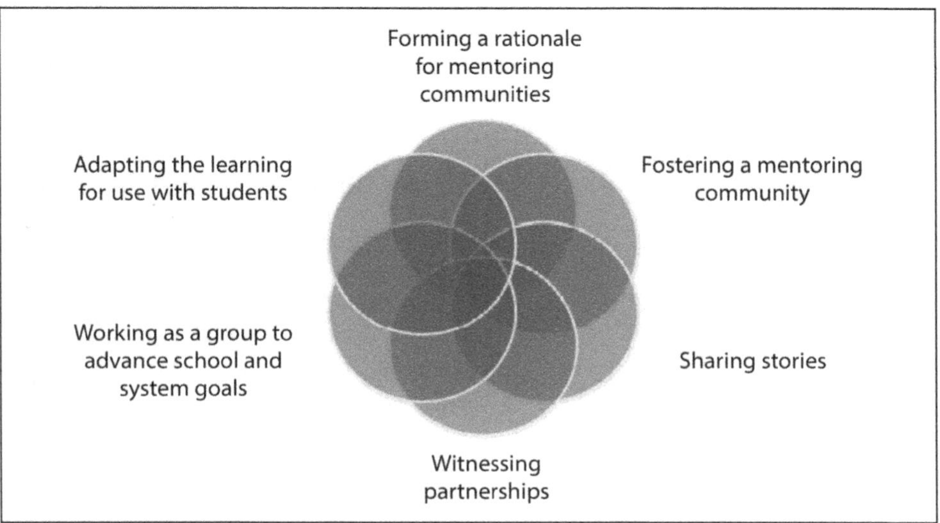

When creating a mentoring community, consider these key questions:

- Why should we endeavor to form mentoring communities? (See page 109.)
- How do we begin to build a mentoring community? (See page 112.)
- How might storytelling contribute to mentoring communities? (See page 114.)
- How might witnessing strengthen partnerships? (See page 117.)
- How might mentoring communities enable progress toward school and system goals? (See page 119.)
- How might the strategies I use with my mentoring community be implemented with the students in my classroom? (See page 122.)

Why should we endeavor to form mentoring communities?

Benefits of Mentoring Communities

As teachers, we would agree that teaching is a lot of work. Therefore, throughout this book, we have advocated for a form of mentoring that can lighten the load. It is in this same spirit that we advocate for mentoring communities. It's true that they can initially require extra effort to organize and coordinate, but we believe that the benefits are so vast they make all the initial effort worthwhile. These benefits, directly observed in our research, include less isolation, exponential knowledge-building, exposure to different perspectives, and the natural development of a growth mindset.

Less Isolation

When working in a community, isolation falls away as new connections and relationships within and among schools become possible. For example, when we brought preservice and induction mentors together for professional development, we observed them making connections, sharing information, following one another's Twitter accounts, and planning to join future professional learning sessions together. The mentors we observed weren't isolated teachers to begin with, as they had mentees. And yet there was something profoundly important about a group of mentors having an opportunity to connect without their mentees present. They were able to share experiences, discuss challenges, identify common themes, offer strategies, and have direct discussions about their mentoring approaches as well as their classroom pedagogy.

Stories from the Field: Ellen's Mentoring Group (Diane and Lana)

In one of our research groups, a cohort of mentor teachers from the same school sat together over the course of a two-day professional development session. On the first day of the session, we overhead Ellen exclaim to one of her colleagues, "Oh, my goodness, I didn't even know you had a teacher candidate!" It turned out that despite four teacher candidates being placed at the same location, none of the mentors realized that other teachers were hosting mentees. As the first day drew to a close, several of the mentors stayed behind. Sitting around the table, they began to discuss a plan for how their school could create a Mentoring Handbook for the upcoming year so that all teachers participating in the work could have a resource as well as a sense of connection to a common project.

This window into our research illustrates the power of a single meeting as a community. The group was moved into action by virtue of their shared values and commitment. They not only solidified their identities as mentors; they also actively planned for their future in a mentoring community. They demonstrated how our knowledge can grow exponentially when we come together.

Exponential Knowledge-Building

In Chapter 2 on Reciprocal Learning, we describe a non-hierarchal learning structure that can produce greater learning outcomes. Here we note that, when mentoring dyads come together, the learning outcomes are stretched in new ways through conversations about common concerns. When one of our mentoring pairs started talking about the challenges of their particular classroom, the nearest pair group had ideas and strategies to share. Instead of progressing along a linear pathway, the learning was taken into new directions by teachers who had similar, yet different, perspectives.

Different Perspectives

One of the benefits of professional learning is the exposure it offers to different ways of solving a problem. This is particularly valuable in a mentoring context for two reasons. First, because the mentor often experiences pressure to provide the "right" answer to their mentee; having more than one mentor and mentee involved in the discussion removes the pressure of certainty and expertise from the shoulders of one mentor and disseminates it into the group. The second reason it is valuable to encounter multiple perspectives while in a mentoring relationship is that being in a community inherently recognizes that there is more than one way to accomplish a desired outcome. A mentor may have one point of view, depending on previous life experience, bias, and belief. A different mentor might have another perspective to offer a mentee that provokes a new way of seeing the situation.

Growth Mindset

A multiplicity of viewpoints leads to more good ideas and less rigid thinking about "right" and "wrong." Some of the most valuable learning a mentee (or a mentor, for that matter) can do is recognizing that the pursuit of correct pedagogy, perfect practice, and the one best way is misplaced. There is no single good way to teach. And the more a mentee hears about how different teachers with varying life backgrounds and differing amounts of experience in the classroom respond to challenges, the broader and more inclusive that mentee's future practice is likely to be.

Mentoring Move: Valuing Community

Community Is Key

"[Coming together] helped develop a stronger sense of community and helped us realize that we, as student teachers and [mentor teachers] are not alone."
—Teacher Candidate, 2017

- Teaching can be lonely, and mentoring can be a first step in opening our professional selves to new connections. In this Mentoring Move, we encourage you to grow those connections even further as a way of realizing some of the benefits of being together.
- This Mentoring Move introduces new dynamics to an established or emerging partnership by extending the conversation into groups. It also provides an opportunity for two levels of conversation: problem-solving for the case study and debriefing the value of the group discussion using the four benefits as conversational touchstones.

3 Simple Steps

1. Before: Each mentor and mentee partnership writes up a small case study that identifies a challenge they are experiencing in their classroom(s). What's happening? What's the concern? What would you like to have happen?
2. During: Come together in a foursome (or more) to discuss your cases. Share ideas, perspectives, and strategies.
3. Debrief: Each mentor and mentee uses the charts on the Valuing Community template on page 126 to document and discuss their experience of the conversation. List examples from the conversation that are evidence of
    - something that made you feel less isolated
    - something that built on or added to your knowledge

See page 126 for the Valuing Community template.

- something that provided a different perspective
- something that encouraged a growth mindset

Discuss each example. Why it was important? How did you feel?

Next Steps

- If your partnership benefitted from the group interactions, consider developing one-off meetings into a structured mentoring community, using Mentoring Move: Planning Community on page 113 to guide you.
- Consider experimenting with another short-term group engagement, which could be productively centred in inquiry using Mentoring Move: Inquiring Collaboratively on page 76 or Mentoring Move: I'd Like to Learn More About… on page 68.

How do we build a mentoring community?

Building a Mentoring Community

Communities aren't just collections of people or, in this case, a collection of partners. Communities can be anchored in time and place through virtual and real-world connections. They are organized around common interests or a common purpose. They come together with intention and adopt practices that benefit all members. A mentoring community is comprised of mentors and mentees. This group can consist of preservice, induction, administrative, and related mentor/mentee groups, who demonstrate the spectrum of learning that teachers progress through as they graduate from universities and continue to teach and lead in various districts.

When developing a mentoring community, think about who will be involved, what you wish to accomplish, when you can come together, where you can meet, and how you will organize the sessions.

- *Who will be involved?* If you are a mentor teacher at your school, look to begin your community locally. Are other teachers at your school mentors? Are there other types of mentoring partnerships who might benefit from joining? Think about preservice and induction educators, teaching assistants, and administrators. If you are an administrator or district lead hoping to coordinate a community, contact your local schools or check with the district to learn if there is already a formal mentoring program. Sometimes there may be existing resources, including a curriculum of sorts, professional development supports, funding, and release time.
- *What do we want to accomplish?* Determining this is perhaps the most important component of the planning process. Mentoring communities might focus on a particular area of need that your school/district has identified; for example, induction mentors and their mentees might meet in the second year of their partnership to learn about collaborative inquiry and to research an issue that is relevant to their classrooms. Or mentoring communities might organize around a particular element of the mentoring relationship; for example, mentors and mentees might come together to explore the mentoring process or to deepen reciprocal learning. To increase participation, buy-in, and authenticity, it is a good idea to set the objective of the community in consultation with the members you intend to invite. Mentoring communities might also develop learning around a chapter in this book that reflects the needs and/or interests

of your community, using the Mentoring Moves as structures to signpost the professional learning.

- *When can we come together?* There is no single best answer for this. We have found that meeting even twice in an academic year can make a real difference. Be realistic about your time and availability. When starting out, it might be helpful to decide to meet once in the fall and once in the spring. Leave enough time between meetings to try some of the strategies and ideas that you have explored, so that you can report your observations and findings back to the group. Very few districts have funding for mentor and mentee release days (funded release from the classroom for learning). Investigate if this is a possibility for your group. If not, schedule your meetings at a common lunch hour or at the end of the day.
- *Where can we meet?* This seems like a relatively straightforward question. However, in the age of MOOCs (massive open online courses) and online learning communities, one of your first decisions will have to be whether the meetings will be in person, fully online, or in a blended environment. While we advocate for in-person meetings whenever possible, we acknowledge that this might not be possible when there are financial, time, and geographic constraints.
- *How should we organize the sessions?* Once you have answered the preceding questions, you can plan the learning. A first step is to refer back to your identified objectives: What are the learning goals? If your objective is to facilitate conversations, it is good to begin with open questions that will encourage discussion and sharing. If your objective is to focus on new theories or learning, you might begin by finding relevant literature (readings, industry texts, videos, guest speakers). With questions and/or learning resources ready, you can determine a flow for each of the sessions. Refer back to some of the themes and Mentoring Moves in this text: How might they support the learning? Try to use a praxis approach: *praxis* means bringing theory into practice, learning into action. Balance theoretical learning with practical strategies and activities. Make ties back to classroom, school, and district objectives. Leave the day's learning with a commitment to next steps, so that the follow-up meeting continues to develop a learning trajectory.

A mentoring community is a variation of professional learning community and it affords opportunities for both growth and leadership. Participating mentors and mentees will have considerable opportunity to share their findings with the school and the district, perhaps inspiring other ad-hoc communities. We know of districts where burgeoning grassroots communities become so plentiful that their learning provided the impetus for the district to develop formal program supports and offer funding.

Mentoring Move: Planning Community

Planning Is Key

"I thought it was really great that we created a safe space for open conversations."
—Teacher Candidate, 2017

- Before planning in earnest, consider what resources your district already has in place. A district might already have professional learning communities organized around key objectives or areas of focus. Districts might also have programming and funding available to support various mentoring contexts. For example, districts we have worked with have established curriculum in support of newly inducted teachers and newly promoted administrators.

- While organizing the community details, don't forget to give thought to how to establish group norms. It isn't simply a question of what you will explore, but also how you will engage with one another.

3 Simple Steps

1. Touch base with administrators at the school and district level to see what's already in place, what might be feasible, and how to mobilize supports.
2. Designate and meet with a small team who will coordinate the efforts. Use the organizer on the Planning Community template on page 127 to help you attend to the major questions.
3. Revisit the plan after the first mentor community meeting to incorporate feedback and make changes.

See page 127 for the Planning Community template.

Next Steps

- Once you have a mentoring community up and running, you can consider ways of incorporating traditional learning models and action research. Mentoring Move: Scaling Questions on page 96 might help, as might Mentoring Move: Inquiring Collaboratively on page 76.
- If your mentoring community has largely focused on in-school mentoring, look for opportunities for community partnerships with local universities and colleges, as well as with other school districts.

Sharing Stories

How might storytelling contribute to mentoring communities?

To really understand the value of a mentoring community, it is helpful to relate it to the social constructivist model of learning. Social constructivism was first developed by Lev Vygotsky (1978), who theorized that learning arises from social interactions and is tied to their context. Learning happens when people, with existing funds of knowledge and identities, come together to share their ideas and discuss perspectives. Learning is not isolated and individualistic; it cannot exist as something to perfect and memorize. This book has indicated that we are advocates for this model of learning. We noted in Chapter 3: Reciprocal Learning that hierarchies are damaging to the learning process; social constructivism assumes reciprocity. In Chapter 1 we argued against modelling best practice in favor of authentic mentoring processes; this is in keeping with a social constructivist approach to learning that states that perfect knowledge does not exist in isolation of context.

It is fitting that, as we advocate for mentoring communities, we propose storytelling as a complementary tool. Storytelling helps community members share learning, build knowledge, develop relationships, and challenge beliefs. It does not ask community mentors and mentees to demonstrate their expertise; rather, it invites each member to feel as though they have something to contribute based on their existing knowledge and experience.

Stories from the Field: Our Most Significant Mentoring Relationships (Diane and Lana)

Lana's Story: Shadow Mentoring

The mentoring relationship that had the most impact on my career was an informal one that began when I first started teaching. My "mentor" was a teacher down the hall who had been teaching for one year more than I had. At first, she, like many of the other teachers on staff, popped by to welcome me to the school and to offer help if I had any questions. It was a nice offer, but I was too new and overwhelmed to take her up on it.

As the first week unfolded, I learned that she taught my class a few different subjects. I also noticed, after several weeks, that my class returned from their time with her in good spirits, energetic, and happy. I began to wonder about her pedagogy and her approach. I began to wonder about how she created such strong relationships with students. And I began to wonder how I might learn from her—not just about planning, instruction and assessment, but also about how to be with students. Over the year, I engaged in what might be called *shadow mentoring*: I paid attention to how she spoke to students in the hallway; I watched her interact with her own class during assemblies and on field trips. I learned from her almost by osmosis.

Eventually, at the start of my second year at the school, I approached her and asked if we could partner to plan some units. I continued to learn from and with her for the next five years that we worked together. Although she was never a formal mentor, we did engage in reciprocal learning for a long time. I think her mentorship had one of the most significant impacts on my practice because I realized that, if I had stayed a shadow mentor, I would have learned about how she interacted with students through observations, but I would have missed the rich understanding of both why and how she made certain choices. It was only once we came together in reciprocal learning that I was able to fully understand her values, beliefs, and practices.

Diane's Story: Coming into Knowing

I came to elementary teaching after a number of years of teaching English as a Second Language in the Canadian military. I was a "mature" novice in the elementary teaching environment, and my mentor teacher was much younger than I was. She was energetic, dynamic, and a real inspiration to me. She engaged with her students as individuals that she got to know well as learners and as people. When I arrived in her classroom for my first practicum, she asked me about my prior experiences and we shared stories that had had impact on us as teachers and learners. I recognized and valued her experience, and she reciprocated. We had much to learn from each other.

Looking back on this time, the significance lies not only in what she taught me but also in how she did so. She rarely gave me advice, but asked me thoughtful questions that led me to analyze and assess my own practice. She shared her ideas and her resources, but was still open to new ideas and experiences that I brought from my faculty studies and my prior work experience. Writing this story, I am reminded that I should get in touch with her to say hello and thank her again for her wisdom and support in helping me to relaunch my career in a new field of education.

Coming together as mentors and sharing our stories, we realized that we had similar experiences as mentees, mentors, and as facilitators. As our research questions emerged organically from our storytelling, we have both first-hand experience and research data to support the value of storytelling to create learning pathways. In our research, for example, we observed how storytelling between mentors created immediate bonds and connections over similar mentoring experiences. The value of stories really became clear when mentors used them to describe their classrooms. Because a story is not simply a report of the facts, it provides a more complete picture of both the context and the storyteller. Storytellers animate their stories with emotional color. They talk about the sequence of events, digress into historical anecdotes, and provide parenthetical insights that illuminate their thoughts and beliefs. They shape their stories for their audience, forging connections and offering differing points of view. Storytellers are the experts in their stories, but that doesn't mean that the storyteller cannot learn through the telling, discussion, and retelling.

Mentoring Move: Storytelling

Being in the Moment Is Key

"Hearing other success stories, but also where other partnerships were struggling or needed help—It made me think about how I could approach difficult situations I encountered."
—Mentor Teacher, 2017

- When was the last time you wrote a story? When did you last tell a story? Was it a story about your classroom? Stories capture the detail and texture of our classroom experiences. The narrative we choose, the central details, and the emotional inflection reveal how we think, feel, and act as educators.
- Note that we are not telling stories to criticize or indict our colleagues, students, and parents. Be intentional in choosing a story that is not "telling tales" of "bad behavior." If there are challenging components in your story, think about how you can share them thoughtfully and reflectively, without assigning blame. Also, be attentive to protecting the privacy of those in the story by changing names and dates as needed.

3 Simple Steps

See page 128 for the Storytelling template.

1. Close your eyes and think deeply about a memorable classroom or teaching experience. Reflect on why this memory stands out: What happened? How did you feel? What was the impact?
2. Find a quiet place. Use the Storytelling template on page 128 to write your story. Include as much detail as possible.
3. Share your story with your mentee and with your mentor community. Discuss what resonates with you after telling the story. Explore how the group responds. Make note of conversational shifts: What questions arise? What new stories are told in response? What new perspectives are offered? Does telling the story change you, as the storyteller?

Next Steps

- Good storytelling begets good storytelling. And storytelling knits a group together over time. If this Mentoring Move produces rich conversations, consider including it as an introductory activity in future professional development contexts.
- Consider how this Mentoring Move can be adapted for classroom use with your students. How do the two components (i.e., writing the story and analyzing what it was like to tell the story) relate to your curriculum? How can they

help students develop new ways of thinking about narrative writing in particular, and about complex content in general?

How might witnessing strengthen partnerships?

Strengthening Partnerships through Witnessing

Witnessing in a mentoring community introduces a new element to the idea of reciprocity. Essentially, witnessing occurs when a mentor and mentee dyad is able to watch another mentor partnership in action. One pair discusses a problem while the second pair observes, making notes on the process. The two pairs might take turns solving problems, discussing case studies, engaging in co-planning, or debriefing a lesson. Witnessing is a particular structure within mentoring communities that builds on the benefits of those communities, including reducing isolation, exponential knowledge-building, and encountering new perspectives. The goal of witnessing is twofold: the first has to do with content; the second has to do with characteristics of the relationship.

Content

When we witness another dyad engage in problem-solving, we become aware of other ways of resolving the problem. We learn new content. A mentor and mentee who listen closely to another partnership's conversation might learn new strategies, increase their awareness of school and district policies, and extend their original understanding of a topic. No matter how experienced a mentor teacher is, there is always something new to learn; witnessing allows that new learning to happen in an authentic context, without overt vulnerability. Witnessing also helps a mentee learn new ways of questioning by overhearing how a different mentee responds to the discussion. A mentee might not know what to ask about or might have a particular mindset when framing their questions. Listening to another mentee helps them to open new pathways of inquiry.

Characteristics

A second goal is of this strategy is to be witness to the process, language, mannerisms, and emotions underpinning someone else's conversation as a way of understanding the qualities that animate their relationship. Self-reflection is difficult, especially when it comes to some of the intangibles of relationship-building. We don't often see ourselves through another's eyes, even when we try. Witnessing offers insight into a different partnership and this insight functions as both a window and a mirror. It is a window into how another dyad talks to one another; how they listen; how they cultivate a demeanor. It is also a mirror: as we watch, we begin to wonder about our own actions and reactions. We ask ourselves, through private and gentle comparisons, how our own mentor/mentee interactions differ. We become aware of new strengths and new areas for ongoing improvement within our mentoring relationship.

Stories from the Field: Listening to Listening about Classroom Management (Lana)

In one of our research sessions, mentors and mentees sat in partnership groups to debrief some Frequently Asked Questions. One question that came up repeatedly was how to develop "classroom management skills." Mentees in the teacher education program would frequently complain that the program didn't teach them how to "manage" student behavior, so it was no surprise when this was raised as a pressing question in our community meeting.

I sat on the periphery of a group of four comprised of two mentor partnerships. I noticed that one dyad was talking about classroom management while the other dyad seemed to be listening. The first pair were talking about how to address and resolve behavioral issues in the classroom. The mentor asked the mentee to provide a specific example from the past week that they could analyze. The mentee mentioned an issue with a particular student who was behaving disruptively. The mentor paused. She leaned back in her chair. She sighed. And then she began talking about the student, his background, and their relationship. She spoke at length about how she didn't really think of classroom management as a function of teacher control. She talked about her own struggles as a child with Attention Deficit Disorder and how that informed the attentiveness and compassion she tried to bring to her classroom. As she spoke, I made observations about her mentee's responses. But I also noticed the other mentor and mentee, listening and making notes. I noted their expressions of interest, surprise, and curiosity.

As researchers, when we reflected on this interaction between the two mentor/mentee pairs, we couldn't help but to think about the potential of these dyadic foursomes. Could we be more intentional about crafting opportunities for these partnerships to listen, with purpose, to one another? The value of hearing someone else articulate their beliefs, describe their approach, and share their strategies authentically generated new perspectives and discussions. In these small groups of four, this happened without it becoming intimidating and high-stakes, and without losing some of the intimacy of a partnership.

So let's take a closer look at what we mean by witnessing and how we can build witnessing into our mentor community. First, is useful to note that witnessing is inherently non-judgmental. When we come together to witness one another's work or process, we are inviting new learning, not sitting in judgment of how the differences are "wrong" or problematic. Second, the purpose of witnessing is to understand how someone else approaches a problem, situates a rationale, and roots their teaching decisions. For this, we should pay attention to the content (e.g., "What tools does this person use to resolve this issue?") as well as the characteristics of their mentor/mentee interaction (e.g., "How does this person position their thinking? Invite discussion? Engage in disagreement?"). The third and final element to consider is that witnessing requires listening as well as some degree of self-reflection. As we reflect on both the content and the characteristics, we should begin to think about our own classroom practices and mentoring strategies. How does this new learning invite us to make changes?

Mentoring Move: Witnessing

"Hearing other opinions/views and collaborating with other mentors helped us progress professionally to be more effective mentors in the future."
— Mentor Teacher, 2017

Listening Is Key

- Witnessing requires us to become observant listeners in a fairly intimate context. To listen observantly, you are tasked with listening for content as well as observing reactions. Your first objective, then, is to suspend your instinct to judge or criticize.
- Witnessing is an invitation to be together and to pay attention to how people connect, establish trust, and express care. It asks you to be outward-looking, present in the conversation as a listener to another mentor/mentee partnership. It also requires you to be inward-looking, as you reflect on your practices and reactions, and question yourself.

3 Simple Steps

See page 129 for the Witnessing template.

1. Meet with another mentoring pair. Listen as they discuss a current problem of practice. The topic can be decided in advance or can emerge organically out of recent experiences.
2. You and your mentee can each use the Witnessing template on page 129 to document your witnessing. Make a note of the content, make observations about the characteristics of their interactions, and reflect on the implications for your own beliefs, values, and practices.
3. Switch roles so that the other mentoring pair has a chance to observe you and your mentee in conversation. Debrief your charts in pairs or, if preferred, as a group.

Next Steps

- This Mentoring Move can be used in complement with Mentoring Move: Storytelling on page 116 during a staff meeting or in an already-established professional learning community.
- It can also be combined with Mentoring Move: Third Points on page 71 to anchor the conversation.

Advancing School and System Goals

How might mentoring communities enable progress toward school and system goals?

When we move mentoring out of the dyadic context and into communities, we automatically create an opportunity to scale learning. In fact, we are hard-pressed to think of a professional development topic that cannot be explored as part of a mentoring community. There are two ways to link professional development and mentoring. One is to gather mentor/mentee pairs from an existing program (e.g., induction mentors, teacher candidates from a teaching program and their associate, host teachers) to engage in learning on a particular topic. For example, one district we work with organizes professional learning for induction mentors and mentees in the areas of literacy, numeracy, assessment, and differentiated instruction.

Another way is to work backward and create professional development contexts that allow mentoring relationships to emerge. For example, if administrators are planning professional development for a staff meeting, we would encourage them to think about creating mentoring partnerships or groups as a way of organizing the learning community. This might mean asking for pairs based on the traditional years-of-experience criterion, but it could also mean organizing mentors around previous teaching experience or areas of interest and expertise. Here are some examples of how this could work:

- A temporary mentoring community could be built across a series of professional development days or over the course of several staff meetings; an administrator might invite five or six teachers passionate about literacy or numeracy practice (or assessment, educational technology, etc) to engage with a small mentoring group of similarly disposed or simply curious colleagues.
- A more long-term community could be used as an organizing structure for an entire school year of staff meetings, with rotating topics as well as rotating group mentors.
- A temporary mentoring community might emerge from a book group that reads a professional text and then shares it with staff during staff meetings or even in district-wide videos and podcasts.
- A longer-term district-wide mentoring community could be sustained in an environment of teachers as researchers, wherein teachers would engage in collaborative inquiry or another research format to inquire, experiment, share, and revise practice.

Two characteristics distinguish this idea of mentoring as a structure for professional learning from simply leading small groups in professional development. First, mentoring requires that a relationship be built and sustained. The learning should take place over time, and not be restricted to one-offs or a single session. Also, in keeping with the importance of reciprocal learning, the mentor would not simply be downloading information to the group, but would engage in sharing, analysis, and planning next steps. If we remove the expectation that the mentoring relationship requires a huge gulf between years of experience, then we create more opportunities for lateral and reciprocal learning.

Stories from the Field: One District's Mentoring Communities (Diane and Lana)

One district we worked with in our research had developed a strategy to engage newly inducted teachers and their mentors in multi-year mentoring communities. This district apportioned some funding each year toward professional development sessions that offered support to mentors, engaged mentors and mentees in professionally mediated co-learning, and sustained the relationships beyond the first year using collaborative inquiry. The district offers different kinds of sessions:

- In formal professional development for induction mentors, mentors are invited to three professional development sessions (fall, winter, and spring) to learn and develop mentoring mindsets and strategies.
- Induction mentors have the opportunity to earn the title of Mentor Leaders through ongoing learning. These Mentor Leaders become centres of influence in their schools and districts, and are able to work with smaller teams of mentors on the further development of mentoring skills and knowledge.
- Formal professional development options are offered for mentor/mentee pairs, organized on topics that are relevant and timely in the district. These sessions might include full-day co-learning sessions on differentiating instruction, literacy and numeracy, assessment and evaluation, modern learning and educational

technology, and more. These sessions offer an opportunity to engage in reciprocal learning for the mentoring pairs, as both the mentor and mentee explore new literature and contribute ideas.

- Induction mentors and their mentees are invited in the second year of partnership to return for a year-long collaborative inquiry engagement. Mentors and their mentees (now in their second year of teaching with the district) attend three professional development sessions (fall, winter, and spring) run by Mentor Leaders. In the first session, the group learns about collaborative inquiry as a research structure. In the second session, they develop a research plan based on a mutual question or problem of practice. In the third session, the pairs return to share the results of their experiments and learning with the whole group. This commitment to a second year of co-learning gives the district an opportunity to facilitate learning about collaborative inquiry, which encourages an ongoing mindset of teacher as researcher. The second year of co-learning demonstrates a commitment to relationship- and network-building, as the partnerships are given ongoing support in both their interpersonal relationship and as a member of a larger community.

Mentoring Move: Scaling Learning pairs well with Mentoring Move: Planning Community.

If your district would like to develop mentoring communities in order to scale learning, we recommend dedicating some time at the outset to discussing the value of relationships, explicitly engaging with mentoring knowledge and skills, and establishing the context for reciprocal learning before proceeding to content learning. To support this, you can refer back to Mentoring Moves from Chapter 1: Building Relationships, Chapter 2: Knowledge and Skills, and Chapter 3: Reciprocal Learning.

Mentoring Move: Scaling Learning

Strategizing Is Key

"[Experience with mentoring] has helped me see that students are caring, and helps me improve my own learning [and] revisit ideas."
—Mentor Teacher, 2017

- When developing a mentoring community to scale learning, or when bringing district learning to a mentoring community, organizers have to be strategic about how to construct opportunities for learning in ways that maintain the value of relationships. This means that the community must have both time and space to come together.
- Organizers also have to be attentive to creating the conditions for mentoring and reciprocal learning before moving ahead to scale learning of content.

3 Simple Steps

1. The first step is to decide if you will be creating and sustaining a new mentoring community in order to engage in professional development, or if you will be bringing content to an existing community. A great place to begin planning is in conversation with district learning coaches, who might have a sense of how to plan the learning, as well as knowledge of whether other communities already exist elsewhere in the district.

See page 130 for the Scaling Learning template.

2. Use the Scaling Learning template on page 130 to signpost your vision. This process can be linked to existing school or district improvement plans.
3. Document the learning over the year. What has been accomplished? What has been the impact in schools and classrooms? What are some new directions for future learning?

Next Steps

- Grow the learning across schools and through the district by bringing clusters or nodes of mentoring communities together.
- Share results of the learning with parents and community stakeholders.

How might the strategies I use with my mentoring community be implemented with the students in my classroom?

Adapting Strategies for Use with Students

Research demonstrates that teachers who engage in mentoring relationships accrue benefits that can transfer to and be transformative in the classroom. Chapter 1's focus on Building Relationships, for example, can be used to cultivate teacher/student and student/student relationships. Some of the ideas that help make our thinking visible from Chapter 2 can be directly adapted to classrooms. And certainly, several of the themes and Mentoring Moves from Chapter 3 on Reciprocal Learning can be tweaked to produce new learning experiences for students.

Stories from the Field: "Transferable Stuff!" (Diane and Lana)

As we worked with mentor teachers and mentees, a common thread ran through feedback and observations: Teachers frequently commented on how much of their learning from mentoring professional development could be transferred to their classrooms. In one group, the teacher candidates took pictures of Mentoring Move: Sharing Values and were overheard discussing how they could adapt the activity for their upcoming placement with students. One of the mentor teachers reflected, "The Values activity, I could do that with my kids. How awesome would that be? Transferable stuff!" Yet another mentor teacher commented that some of the work we were doing to dismantle conventional hierarchies should also be at the heart of their work with students.

While our research did not intentionally emphasize classroom connections, it wasn't surprising to us that the learning naturally flowed into student contexts. After all, as teachers, we place a tremendous amount of emotional value in feeling what it is like to be a learner again. It makes us more empathetic to student experiences, as our own learning can feel enriching and empowering, or frustrating and minimizing. We become mindful of how difficult it is to sit and receive. And most importantly for this book, we are reminded of the value of meaningful, purposeful conversation.

For these reasons, we spend the remainder of this chapter examining Mentoring Moves from previous chapters that can be revised and mobilized in classrooms. We provide some overarching analysis on the context and the benefits of using these Moves with students.

Learning Move: Making Connections

From Chapter 1, page 11

Making Connections is endlessly adaptable for the classroom.

- The cube and six prompts can be designed to cultivate community with a new group of students in September.

- The prompts can be aimed at particular content as a mid-unit review or as a way of drawing out existing knowledge before beginning a unit.
- The cube can be given students who can choose to incorporate their own prompts or questions.
- Finally, we love the cube as a tool for encouraging metacognitive thinking: a teacher can rewrite the prompts to encourage students to share their thought process for learning or problem-solving.

See page 131 for Making Connections: Student Metacognition, a template that has been modified in preparation for self-assessment and can also be used for peer feedback.

The benefits include facilitating conversation using prompts as scaffolds for learning, increased engagement, and multiple entry points for oral language development in second-language learners and in students with communication exceptionalities.

Learning Move: Needs Analysis

From Chapter 2, page 52

See page 59 for the Needs Analysis template.

Needs Analysis is a great technique to check understanding of new or complex content. In lieu of providing a graphic organizer, we recommend creating a virtual or chart paper three-column table using the three categories from the Needs Analysis template on page 59. This can be used as an entry or minds-on activity for students as they start class, or as a consolidation activity at the end of class. Students write a question on a sticky note (or as a virtual entry) based on learning from the previous class. They choose which category they feel it belongs: Pressing Question for key comprehension questions; Wondering About for clarifications; and Nice to Chat About as opportunities for extension. If the teacher prefers to maintain student privacy, then instead of posting their questions to a central organizer, students can code their questions as Pressing, Wondering, or Extending.

Benefits include receiving student feedback about areas that might need reteaching or clarification, determining opportunities for extension, and perhaps even preparing short-term mixed-ability groupings.

Learning Move: Stoplight Self-Assessment

From Chapter 2, page 50

This move uses the stoplight colors to self-assess progress toward a goal.

Refer to the Stoplight Self-Assessment template on page 58.

- Students can use this approach as a mid-unit or mid-project check-in to determine which areas they have developed adequately, what needs more work, and what might need teacher assistance. Students review their work alongside the success criteria and highlight the criteria using red, yellow, and green to denote their progress. A key element for this Mentoring Move is to have established success criteria that students understand.
- The stoplight can also be inverted into a scavenger hunt. Ask students to identify one area of their project or paper that is green (clearly meets the requirements of certain success criteria), one element that they are still working on that is yellow (is in the process of moving toward success criteria), and one element where they need further support that is red.

The benefits of either technique include reminding students of the criteria, preparing students to reflect upon and discuss their progress with peers or teachers in conferences, and narrowing the focus for next steps.

Learning Move: What I Bring

From Chapter 3, page 63

This Learning Move dovetails nicely with Learning Move: Making Connections on page 122. As an organizer, the tree suggests plurality and connectedness; that is, the tree offers students a way to express their diverse perspectives, experiences, and backgrounds, while also rooting them in the shared space of the classroom. This Learning Move, as in the example for mentoring, can be centred on a conversation about the gifts we bring into spaces and relationships. In this case, the tree visually depicts the gifts students bring to the classroom. The concept that animates What I Bring is recognizing that we all contribute uniquely. Students can use the tree to respond to the question "What gifts do I bring to our classroom community?" or "What makes me a good friend and classmate?"

The key benefit of this Learning Move is that it emphasizes that each of us is an individual with something to give. For students, especially in schools where academic performance is the only thing openly valued, this discussion recognizes and validates other elements of their lives.

Learning Move: Sharing Values

From Chapter 3, page 65

Sharing Values is a Learning Move that draws together disparate values and seeks common themes. Reproduce the concentric circles on the Sharing Values, page 1 template on page 79 on chart paper or other large surface for a class brainstorm.

- This strategy can be helpful at the start of the year or at the start of a course for establishing classroom norms. Traditionally, if teachers ask students to co-construct classroom rules, the emphasis is on student behavior; the same is true for teachers who ask students to sign behavior contracts. We suggest that the benefit of this Learning Move is that it draws the discussion away from rules-based compliance and moves it toward a recognition that both teacher and students have roles to play in a classroom's success. It addresses the power dynamic between teachers and students, and provides students with a more complete voice in the development of their spaces.
- This Move can also be adapted to develop norms in advance of co-learning experiences. This might include using it to prepare students for peer assessment or for participating in community circles.

The benefits include drawing students' attention to mindset and behaviors, developing shared language around norms, setting expectations for respectful communication, and encouraging self-reflection and responsibility.

Learning Move: Storytelling

From Chapter 5, page 116

Sharing stories is at the heart of much good classroom practice. Literacy education often begins with picture books and writing stories. As a Learning Move, it provides an additional structure that emphasizes storytelling in addition to story writing. It can be used in language classes, but also in any curricular context where making a connection to a theme is important. For example, a teacher might ask students to write a story about personal and family experiences with migration at the start of a Social Sciences unit.

One benefit of this Learning Move is the focus on reading aloud and listening to each other's stories, rather than on the writing process. An additional benefit is that students can use the questions to explore their own identities as writers.

This is particularly true of the question: How does telling my story change me as the storyteller?

As you work through some of the Moves, you might think of your own new and creative adaptations for the classroom. Have a look through the chapters again: can you identify other Moves that can be tweaked for use with students in your classroom?

Valuing Community

Evidence of...	Mentor
Less isolation	
Knowledge-building	
Different perspective	
Growth mindset	

Evidence of...	Mentee
Less isolation	
Knowledge-building	
Different perspective	
Growth mindset	

Planning Community

	Mentoring Community for ____________________ **(School or district)**	**Next Steps**
Who will be involved?		
What do we want to accomplish?		
When can we come together?		
Where can we meet?		

How should we organize the sessions?	Relevant Mentoring Moves (if applicable)

Pembroke Publishers ©2020 *Mentoring Each Other* by Lana Parker and Diane Vetter ISBN 978-1-55138-346-0

Storytelling

After telling your story, what questions arise?

What new stories are told in response?

What new perspectives are offered?

Is there new learning?

Does telling the story change you, as the storyteller?

Witnessing

Content	Characteristics	Self-reflection
What problem of practice is the partnership discussing?	How do the mentor and mentee engage in discussion?	How do their strategies and ideas connect with my existing practice?
What tools and strategies do the mentor and mentor propose?	How do they engage in disagreement?	What kinds of "talk tools" or ways of interacting do they model that might guide my mentoring relationship?
What kinds of theory and experience seem to inform their decision-making?	How do they ensure that both voices are heard?	What questions do I have?

Scaling Learning

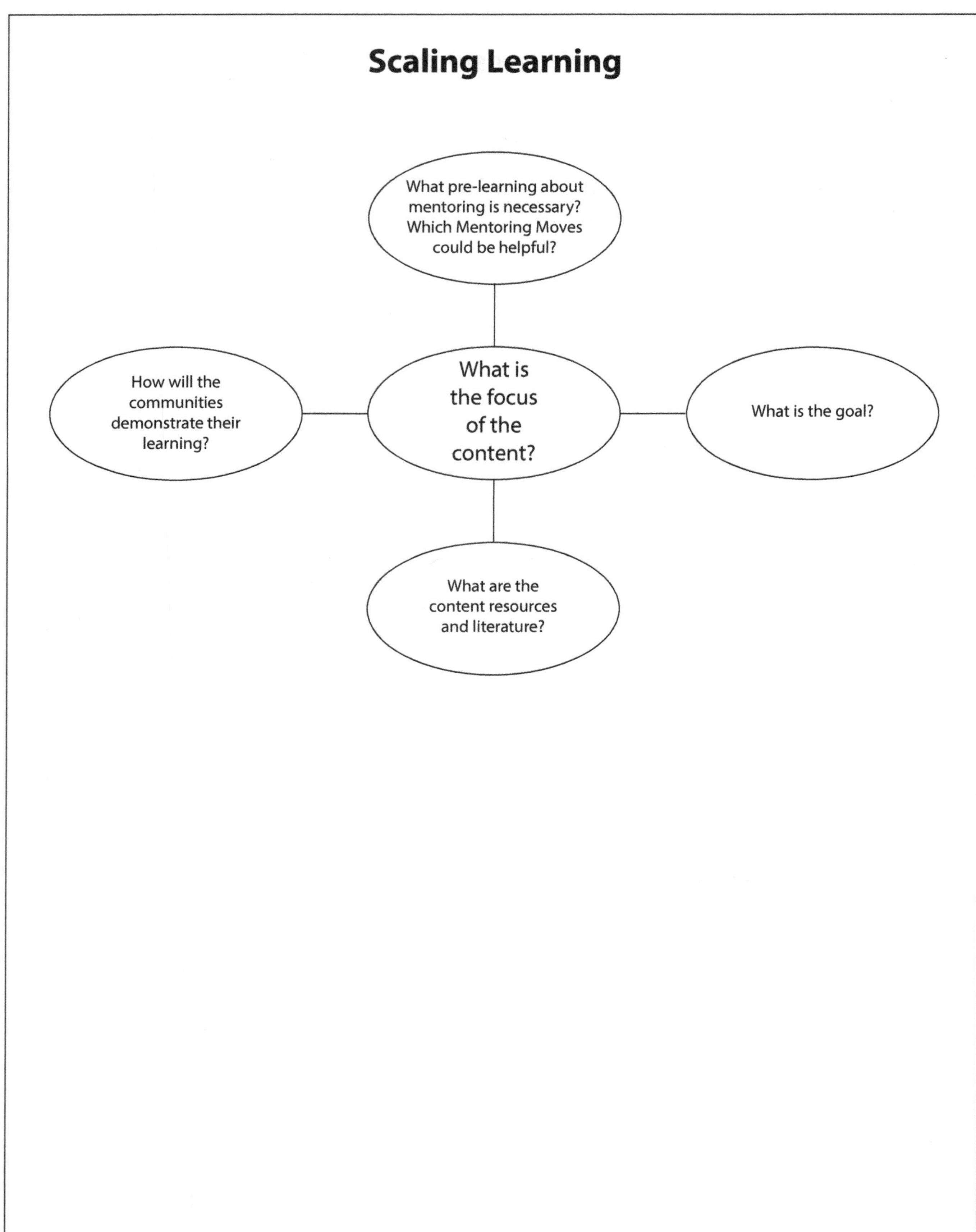

Pembroke Publishers ©2020 *Mentoring Each Other* by Lana Parker and Diane Vetter ISBN 978-1-55138-346-0

Making Connections: Student Metacognition

When I look at this work	I'm proud of…
I connect it to what we learned in class by…	I need to revise…
I want some advice about how to…	I have a question about…

I want to learn more about…

Connections Cube

Print out a connections cube for each group of students. Have them fold and tape or glue into a cube.
Use the 6 starters to design a self-assessment discussion tool.
Students can take turns rolling the cube and talking about their work.

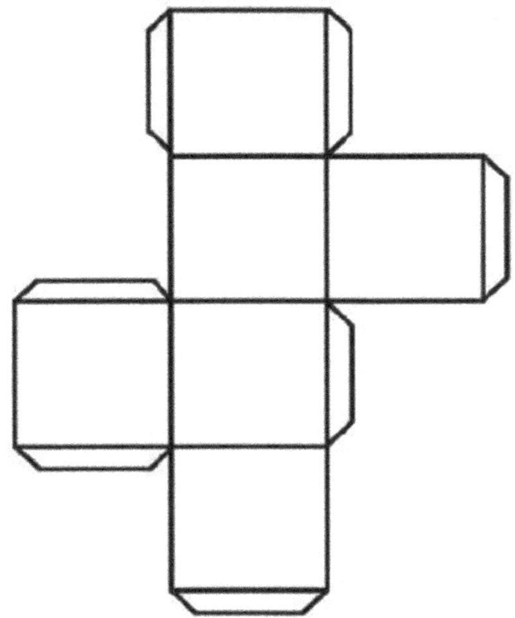

Pembroke Publishers ©2020 *Mentoring Each Other* by Lana Parker and Diane Vetter ISBN 978-1-55138-346-0

Final Thoughts

The authors would like to acknowledge the contribution of our colleague Suzanne Molitor, who collaborated on the original research. We would also like to extend our gratitude to the school districts who hosted our research.

After engaging with the Mentoring Moves and the stories in our book, we hope that you are inspired to continue the journey that views mentoring as a collaborative relationship, in which both mentor and mentee make a commitment to broaden and deepen their knowledge and skills. Mindful of the traditional power dynamics, we hope that your mentoring relationships offer space for reciprocal learning and that, as you develop your identity as a mentor, you experience the role as an expression of learning and leadership. We encourage you to see your mentoring relationships as living within larger communities with the potential to advance professional goals.

The mentoring relationship is at the heart of how we advance in education. In fact, the mentoring relationship is likely at the heart of most organizational learning. Mentors and mentees bring theory to life and invest in themselves as they share their intellectual curiosity, experiences, and hopes for the future.

We hope that your work with the Mentoring Moves helps develop a culture of mentoring each other that extends beyond the boundaries of a conventional relationship and into the classroom. In an ideal world, the desire for responsible and equitable reciprocal learning should animate all relationships, as colleagues mentor colleagues and students mentor each other.

Professional Resources

References

Andreae, G. (2001). *Giraffes Can't Dance.* New York, NY: Scholastic Inc.

Baker, J. W. (2000, April). "The 'Classroom Flip': Using web course management tools to become a guide by the side" Paper presented at the 11th international conference on college teaching and learning, Jacksonville, FL.

Brown, M. W. (1949). *The Important Book.* New York, NY: Harper Collins.

Bryk, A. S. & Schneider, B. (2003). "Trust in Schools: A core resource for school reform" *Educational Leadership*, 60 (6), 40–45.

de Shazer, S. (1994). *Words Were Originally Magic.* New York, NY: W.W. Norton.

Evans, R. (1971). *Richard Evans' Quote Book: Selected from the spoken word and thought for the day and from many inspiring thought-provoking sources from many centuries.* Salt Lake City UT: Latter Day Saints.

Fountas, I. C., & Pinnell, G. S. (2001). *Guiding Readers and Writers Grades 3–6: Teaching comprehension, genre, and content literacy.* Portsmouth, NH: Heinemann.

Gee, J.P. (2008). *Social Linguistics and Literacies: Ideologies in discourses* (3rd ed). New York, NY: Routledge.

Giroux, H. (1994). "Teachers, Public Life and Curriculum Reform" in A.C. Ornstein & L.S. Behar-Horenstein (Eds.) *Contemporary Issues in Curriculum* (2nd ed, pp.36–43). Needham Heights, MA: Allyn and Bacon.

Hyerle, D. (2008). *Visual Tools for Transforming Information into Knowledge.* Thousand Oaks, CA: Corwin.

Kramarski, B., & Michalsky, T. (2009). "Investigating Preservice Teachers' Professional Growth in Self-Regulated Learning Environments" *Journal of Educational Psychology*, 101(1), 161–175.

Lieberman, A., & Miller, L. (2005). "Teachers as Leaders" *The Educational Forum,* 69 (2), 151–162.

Lewis, C. (1982). *Using the "Thinking-aloud" Method in Cognitive Interface Design* (Technical report). IBM.

Molitor, S., Parker, L., Vetter, D. (2018). "Mentoring for All: Building knowledge and community" *Journal of Professional Capital and Community* 3 (4), 242–255

Palmer, P. J. (1998). *The Courage to Teach: Exploring the inner landscape of a teacher's life.* San Francisco, CA: Jossey-Bass,

Timperley, H & Earl, L. (2008). *Professional Learning Conversations: Challenges in using evidence for improvement.* New York, NY: Springer.

Vetter, D. (2008). "Toward a Critical Stance: Citizenship education in the classroom" In M. O'Sullivan & K. Pashby (Eds) *Citizenship Education in the Era of Globalization: Canadian perspectives.* Rotterdam, Netherlands: Sense Publishing.

Vygotsky, L. (1978). *Life in Classrooms.* New York, NY: Teachers College.

Vygotsky, L. (1986). *Thought and Language* (A. Kozulin, Trans.). Cambridge, MA: The MIT Press. (Original work published 1934)

Wiederhold, C. W. (1998). *Cooperative Learning & Higher-Level Thinking: The Q-Matrix.* San Clemente, CA: Kagan Cooperative Learning.

Wiggins, G. & McTighe, J. (1998). *Understanding by Design.* Upper Saddle River, NJ: Merrill Prentice Hall.

Wilhelm, J. (2001). *Improving Comprehension with Think-aloud Strategies: Modeling what good readers do.* New York, NY: Scholastic.

Web Resources

Literacy Information and Communication System. Retrieved from https://lincs.ed.gov/state-resources/federal-initiatives/teal/guide/metacognitive

Oxford Reference Dictionary Retrieved from https://www.oxfordreference.com/view/10.1093/oi/authority.20110803100150570

Index